Improving your Quiet Time

Simon J Robinson

D0756259

DayOne

© Day One Publications 1998
First printed 1998

Scripture quotations are from The New King James Version.
© 1982 Thomas Nelson Inc.

British Library Cataloguing in Publication Data available
ISBN 0 902548 88 3

Published by Day One Publications
3 Epsom Business Park, Kiln Lane, Epsom, Surrey KT17 1JF.
☎ 01372 728 300 **FAX** 01372 722 400
e-mail address: ldos.dayone@ukonline.co.uk

All rights reserved

No part of this publication may be reproduced, or stored in a retrieval system, or transmitted, in any form or by any means, mechanical, electronic, photocopying, recording or otherwise, without the prior permission of **Day One Publications.**

Designed by Steve Devane.
Printed by Clifford Frost Limited, Wimbledon London SW19

Dedicated to Ivy Robinson

Contents

FOREWORD **7**

1 SURVEYING THE CHALLENGE **9**

2 ASSESSING THE NEED **18**

3 GATHERING THE EQUIPMENT **25**

4 NUTS AND BOLTS **34**

5 EXTENDING THE TERRITORY **46**

6 HANDLE WITH CARE **60**

7 A TOUR OF THE TERRAIN **67**

8 SOME FOOTSTEPS TO FOLLOW **84**

9 IT'S GOOD TO TALK **95**

10 THINGS THAT GO BUMP **100**

NOTES **114**

BIBLE READING PLAN **116**

A t Easter I paid a weekend visit to the city where I spent three years as a student in the early 1950s. It was particularly nostalgic to walk along the street where for two years I had digs, remembering the rather formidable landladies we had in those days. I shared with my wife a memory that came uppermost as I pointed out where I stayed. It was of new Christians throwing small stones up at my first floor bedroom window. The object was to attract my attention for me to open the front-door. They came to share a quiet time before breakfast. To ring the bell so early would have disturbed the landlady and to have broken the window would have incurred her wrath even more! Simon Robinson's book 'Improving your Quiet Time' has reminded me again of how important it was, and is, to establish from the very beginning of a person's Christian experience the habit of daily Bible reading and prayer.

I did not hear the gospel until I was in my teens, and had no background of daily Bible reading and prayer. I realise now that from the earliest days of my Christian experience older Christians taught me this practice. Looking back I realise how invaluable the encouragement of that habit was, and the life-time benefit it has been.

A common feature of Christian fellowship during National Service in the Armed Forces in the 1950s was what was known as the Blackboard meeting. The members of the group agreed to read the same Bible reading portions each day—usually from the Scripture Union. Each chose and wrote down a verse, or part of a verse, every day. Then once a week, the members met to compare the verses they had chosen. A verse was voted on for each day, and that went up on the blackboard. Then at the end the group voted on the verse for the week, which became a memory verse. It all helped to establish daily Bible reading and prayer.

The habit of a daily quiet time has the best of precedents, as this book shows. Mark tells us, 'Very early in the morning, while it was still dark, Jesus got up, left the house and went off to a solitary place, where He prayed' (1:35). The Lord Jesus deliberately withdrew not only from the crowds, but also from His disciples, in order to be alone with His Father. His private life was a life of fellowship with His Father. If the Lord Jesus needed quiet times of fellowship and prayer, how much more do we? He died so that we, by the merits of His blood, might have this priceless privilege of free and bold access into our Father's presence. He gave His life and rose again that we might receive the gift of His Spirit to enable us to cry to God, 'Abba, Father!'

The way in which we organise our times of quiet is personal to us, and there are no rules laid down in the Bible. All of us gain, however, from the experience of others. Basic Bible principles need to be constantly restated and reapplied to the circumstances of each new generation. My prayer is that Simon Robinson's helpful and honest sharing of his experience and his eminently practical advice will prompt and encourage many others.

As we take care of our secret life of fellowship with God, our public and private life will not be in conflict and opposition. Instead, our life will show how attractive the gospel of our Lord Jesus Christ is. As we take root below, we bear fruit above.

Derek Prime
Edinburgh

Surveying the Challenge

What is a Quiet Time?

After spending the morning trying to put it out of my mind, the mechanic had rung to tell me that he had found out what was wrong with my car. 'Mr. Robinson' he said, sounding a bit like a doctor who's about to break some bad news. 'I've found the problem; it's your callipers.' I reacted with mixed feelings, I was relieved to hear the problem had been isolated, but I had no idea of what he was talking about, and I had a nasty feeling that whatever a calliper was, it was going to be expensive. I have to admit it—I couldn't muster up the courage to say that I didn't understand what he was telling me! I just asked about the cost, held my breath, and then told him to go ahead with the work.

I am sure that there must be thousands of people who, like me, have little or no idea of the way car engines are put together, but are too embarrassed to ask about the things they don't understand. I wonder how many people feel the same way when they hear other Christians talk about 'quiet times'. That's why I have begun this book by asking 'What is a quiet time?' Those of us who have been Christians for many years may understand the term, but we should not assume that everyone knows what it means. If you are one of the former rather than the latter you might be tempted to move on to the next chapter—please don't! It will do none of us any harm to spend a few moments standing back and giving some thought to the definition of the term 'quiet time.' We may even find that this time-honoured expression will take on a whole new meaning.

If you took a sample of people who are not Christians and asked them for their definition of a quiet time, they probably wouldn't have too much difficulty in providing you with one. They might describe it as a period which is free from disturbance or noise, or as part of the day in which you can allow yourself a little personal space, or a time set aside for 'reflection'. We couldn't really fault any of these responses, each goes part of the way in providing a definition, but none of them gives us the particular distinction that our relationship with God brings to it.

When we talk about a 'quiet time' we are not describing a segment of time that has been set-aside for personal reflection, or a 'quiet corner' in which can take refuge from the onslaught of a busy day. We are describing a distinctive Christian practice, which should be understood within the context of our relationship with God.

The Quiet Time is a part of the day that is given to the worship of God

Worship is a basic word in our Christian vocabulary, yet in this age of 'worship leaders', 'worship tapes', and 'worship songs' the simple meaning of the word can get lost in all the enthusiasm people have for it.

In the Old Testament, 'worship' usually means 'to bow down' or 'to prostrate oneself out of respect'. Sometimes it can mean 'to serve', for example, in the New International Version, Exodus 9:1 says ' Let my people go, so that they may worship me' while the New King James Version says 'let my people go, that they may **serve** me.' The latter is the more accurate translation because the Hebrew word speaks of expressing worship in service to God.

Several Greek words find their way into our English translations of the New Testament as 'worship'. One links worship with our service to God. Another speaks of showing reverence to God, and the most common word is related to the idea of bowing down before God.

Worship is an act of submission to God.

Why do people bow down to a king? They are showing they understand their respective relationship—he is the superior and they are the inferiors. That is why one of the words translated as 'worship' in the Bible is linked to the concept of bowing down before God. When we worship God we acknowledge the fact that He is the King and we are His subjects, that He is our Creator and we are His creation. As the Psalmist says ' Oh come, let us worship and bow down; let us kneel before the LORD our Maker' (Psalm 95:6).

Worship is an expression of our commitment to God.

There is no doubt that the emphasis placed on worship today is a breath of fresh air, but we need to be careful not to separate our worship *of* God from our service *to* God. There is a danger that 'worship' can be seen as the exciting part in which we are keen to be involved, while service is the challenging element which we leave on one side. However, the Old and New Testament forge a direct connection between the two. When we worship God we must realise that we are servants and that we are called to present ourselves as 'living sacrifices, holy and acceptable to God' which is our 'reasonable service' (Romans 12:1). We can't truly worship God if we're not prepared to live for Him.

Worship is a joyful expression of thanksgiving to God.

I was brought up to say 'thank you' for things that were given to me, it was the polite thing to do, but when we give thanks to God we offer more than social politeness. Thanksgiving is an expression of our heartfelt gratitude to God; this serves to sharpen our focus and to put things into perspective. When I was a child our Sunday school class used to sing a song that said 'count your blessings, name them one by one, and it will surprise you what the Lord has done.' These words may have become a little well-worn, but they are true! Thanksgiving enables us to look away from the things that discourage us and to identify the many blessings which God has poured out on us.

We will all have times when our mood or our circumstances make it very difficult to offer this kind of praise to God. When I find myself in this position I turn to the opening verses of a New Testament letter. They usually contain some words of praise for Who God is and what He has done. For example, look at the opening verses of Peter's first letter:

'Blessed be the God and Father of our Lord Jesus Christ, who according to His abundant mercy has begotten us again to a living hope through the resurrection of Jesus Christ from the dead,' (1 Peter 1:3).

The next time you find it difficult to offer joyful thanksgiving to God turn to that verse, spend a moment thinking about it, read it out loud and then thank God for each blessing mentioned. When you do this you will discover a fresh appreciation of the new life God has given you, the blessings He has poured out on you and the future He has planned for you. This will add a whole new dimension to your praise of God and a new appreciation of the work He is doing in your life.

Praising God in a big meeting can be an exhilarating experience. Joining with thousands of others who have the same purpose in mind presents a great incentive to worship, but it can be a very different story when we are on our own, in fact there are times when we will find it very difficult to worship the Lord. One of the most effective ways to overcome this kind of difficulty is to stop and think of what God has done for us and then make it the framework for an expression of worship. This is what David was doing when he said 'Bless the Lord, O my soul and forget not all His benefits' (Psalm 103: 2).

The Quiet Time is a part of the day that is given to the reading of the Word of God

One of the distinctive features of the Bible is the way that it speaks about itself. It describes itself as milk, meat, water, truth, a hammer, a sword, a fire, and a seed. A study of these descriptions alone will show us that it is no ordinary book! The most fitting description for the quiet time depicts the Bible as food. When the people of Israel were gathered on the borders of the Promised Land, they were privileged to hear the final sermon that Moses was to deliver. This great sermon can be found in the book of Deuteronomy. In the course of the book, the children of Israel are reminded of the way in which God fed them with manna while they were in the wilderness. While this satisfied their hunger and met their physical need, it was also designed to keep them humble and to teach them a spiritual lesson. The lesson being that 'man shall not live by bread alone; but man lives by every word that proceeds from the mouth of the LORD (Deuteronomy 8:3). In the same way, the Psalmist said ' How sweet are Your words to my taste, sweeter than honey to my mouth!' (Psalm 119:103).

In the course of a phenomenal vision, God called Ezekiel to be a Prophet; He gave him a scroll (which symbolised His Word) and told him to eat it. This didn't mean that Ezekiel needed to go through his prophetic ministry eating bits of parchment! It was part of a vision in which God was showing Him how he must feed on the very words that were going to be entrusted to him. They had to be part of him if they were going to be proclaimed by him. This has some important things to teach us about the quiet time.

It reminds us that we need to feed on God's Word each day

Food is an essential part of our lives, if we didn't take regular daily meals we would fade away and die. This was the point Moses made when he used the daily provision of manna to remind the Israelites of their need to feed on 'every word that proceeds from the mouth of God'.

It calls for discipline

We have already thought about the vision in which Ezekiel was handed a scroll which he was commanded to eat. In the account that he gives, he observes that 'there was writing on the inside and on the outside, and written on it were lamentations and mourning and woe' (Ezekiel 2:10). When he obeyed the command he found the experience surprisingly agreeable, Ezekiel says that 'it was in my mouth like honey in sweetness' (Ezekiel 3:3). There is no doubt that some parts of the Bible are a lot easier to understand than others. We thrive on the encouragement and the instruction that we can glean from the accounts of Abraham or Joseph. We draw comfort from the deep spirituality expressed through the frail humanity of the Psalmists. On the other hand, some of the visions and oracles we read about in the Prophet's books, or the intricacies of the laws and feasts in Exodus and Leviticus are not quite so easy to read. Nevertheless Ezekiel's experience tells us that even the passages of Scripture we might shrink from, and those that are 'full of lament, mourning and woe' (Ezekiel 2:10), can be food for our souls. Some books in the Bible may appear to be formidable, but we neglect them at our cost. In a verse that we thought about earlier Moses said 'man shall not live by bread alone; but man lives by **every** word that proceeds from the mouth of the Lord' (Deuteronomy 8:3). Similarly Paul told Timothy that' **all** Scripture is given by inspiration of God, and is profitable for doctrine, for reproof, for correction, for instruction in righteousness,' (2 Timothy 3:16). If we take these statements seriously we won't shy away from the parts of the Bible which are harder to understand. To feed on God's Word properly we need to have a balanced diet that incorporates every part of the Bible. This will involve us tackling the books we find more difficult, and that will require discipline. We cannot pretend it will be easy but, if we persist, we will find they will 'taste as sweet as honey' in our mouths (Ezekiel 3:3).

It encourages us to grow

Peter links the idea of feeding on God's Word with spiritual growth. He tells those who are young in the faith to 'desire the pure milk of the Word, that you may grow thereby' (1 Peter 2:2). Paul spoke in similar terms when he addressed the elders of the Church at Ephesus saying: 'I commend you to God and to the word of His grace, which is able to build you up and give you an inheritance among all those who are sanctified' (Acts 20:32). If we neglect the daily provision of God's Word we will stunt our spiritual growth and make little progress in the Christian life.

The Quiet Time is a part of the day that is given to fellowship with God

In these days, the word 'fellowship' has been given a rather elastic meaning. A 'time of fellowship' could describe anything from a barbecue to a Bible study! However, there is nothing vague about the word when it is used in the New Testament. 'Fellowship' is all about participation or sharing, it speaks of a two-way relationship. Paul tells us that God has called us 'into the fellowship of His Son, Jesus Christ' (1 Corinthians 1:9) and John declares that 'our fellowship is with the Father and with His Son, Jesus Christ' (1 John 1:3). 'Fellowship' describes the unique relationship that we have with God through Jesus, which overflows into our relationship with other Christians. This is what makes the quiet time such an exciting prospect—it is not a religious duty but a revolutionary opportunity. We can communicate with our Creator! What could be more exciting than that? But if we are going to explore this magnificent privilege, we will need to equip ourselves with three essential things.

First, we must have **faith in Christ.** John tells us that 'no one has seen God at any time' (1 John 4:12). There is only one way to encounter Him and this is through faith. In fact Hebrews tells us that 'without faith it is impossible to please Him, for he who comes to God must believe that He is, and that He is a rewarder of those who diligently seek Him' (Hebrews 11:6).

One of the greatest examples of faith we have in the Bible is the Old Testament character Abraham, Paul describes him as 'our father' (Romans 4:1) using his experience as a practical example. When the Old Testament speaks of the sort of faith exemplified by Abraham, it describes a 'personal trusting response to God who speaks words of promise'[1]. Abraham demonstrates this in the way he held on to the promise that God had given him until it was fulfilled. The promise in question was initially revealed when God called him to pull up his tent pegs and move on to the place to which he would be sent. God assured him: ' I will make you a great nation; I will bless you and make your name great; and you shall be a blessing' (Genesis 12:2). Years later, God appeared to Abraham in a vision. Abraham took the opportunity to petition Him about the promise that had been made all those years ago.

'But Abram said, "Lord God, what will You give me, seeing I go childless, and the heir of my house is Eliezer of Damascus?" Then Abram said, "Look, You have given me no offspring; indeed one born in my house is my heir!' (Genesis 15:2-3).

God responded to Abraham's prayer by amplifying the promise that He had already made.

And behold, the word of the LORD came to him, saying, "This one shall not be your heir, but one who will come from your own body shall be your heir." Then He brought him outside and said, "Look now toward heaven, and count the stars if you are able to number them." And He said to him, "So shall your descendants be" (Genesis 15:4-5).

The next verse tells us 'Abram believed in the LORD and He accounted it to him for righteousness' and in his letter to the Christians at Rome Paul adds that Abraham ' did not waver at the promise of God through unbelief, but was strengthened in faith, giving glory to God.' (Romans 4:20).

The New Testament develops the idea of faith as 'personal trusting response to God who speaks words of promise'[2]. Our faith is centred on the Lord Jesus and grounded on His death and resurrection. Paul tells us that 'all the promises of God in Him are Yes, and in Him Amen, to the glory of God through us' (2 Corinthians 1:20). Having dealt with our sins at the

Cross and defeated death in His resurrection, Jesus Christ has done everything necessary to bring us back to God. We draw near to God by trusting in all that Christ has done and by believing the promises that He has given us. That is why faith is such an important element of our fellowship with God.

Secondly, if fellowship with God is a two-way process, we will need to cultivate the practice of **listening to God**. This involves us understanding the meaning of the passage that we are reading, perceiving what God is saying to us, and putting it into practice.

My wife tells me that I have 'selective deafness'. She says I have no difficulty in hearing her say 'dinner's ready' while I seem to find it more difficult to hear her when she asks me to tidy the lounge. We can be selective in the way that we listen to what God is saying in His Word. We can seize on the exciting, encouraging verses and sift out the challenging ones. We should not come to God primarily to look for blessing; our first responsibility is to listen to what He is saying to us, and it will be as we hear and obey the Word that we will experience blessing (see James 1:25). There is an old saying that 'God didn't give us two ears and one mouth for nothing'. In order to get the most out of our quiet times we need to be listening to what God is saying in His Word. This will not always be a comfortable experience, because God has a way of exposing sin we must repent of and issuing challenges that we must act upon, and we must not be selective about what we hear.

Thirdly, when we have listened to God we must respond to Him, and we do this through **prayer**. Prayer describes the way in which we are able to speak to our heavenly Father as His children in order to bring our own needs and the needs of others before Him. In his classic book on this subject, O. Hallesby said that prayer should be 'free, spontaneous, vital fellowship between the created person and the personal Creator, in which Life should touch life.'[3] In the light of Hallesby's definition of prayer it is hardly surprising that it should be so important to our fellowship with God and such a vital part of our quiet times.

Prayer should be woven into the fabric of the quiet time. One of the ways that I have cultivated this is that, having meditated on a verse or a passage of scripture, I make it the basis for the initial part of my time of prayer. For example, this morning I was reading Paul's letter to the Corinthians where the apostle says: 'according to the grace of God which was given to me, as a wise master builder I have laid the foundation, and another builds on it. But let each one take heed how he builds on it.' (1 Corinthians 3:10). I discovered this had a lot to say to me as a church leader. After I had spent a little time meditating on the chapter, it became a stimulus for prayer. I prayed about the work God had called me to, asking that He would show me any areas in which it might be shoddy or careless and to grant me the wisdom to know how to correct such things.

I continued to pray along the lines of the following verses in which Paul talks about the way our work will be tested on the day of judgement: 'For no other foundation can anyone lay than that which is laid, which is Jesus Christ. Now if anyone builds on this foundation with gold, silver, precious stones, wood, hay, straw, each one's work will become clear; for the Day will declare it, because it will be revealed by fire; and the fire will test each one's work, of what sort it is.' (1 Corinthians 3:11-13).

This prompted me to ask the Lord what He would think of the quality of my work if He were to return today. Then I went on to pray that I might learn from my mistakes and fulfil my ministry with my eyes fixed on that final test the chapter speaks of. This is an example from my own experience, but I hope it illustrates the way in which we can pray about the things that God has been saying to us in His Word.

I describe this as an initial time of prayer because there will be other things we need to speak to the Lord about. There will be the needs and challenges of the day ahead, our family, our church, our missionary friends, and the world at large. We shall think about these things in more detail later in the book. For the time being we'll remind ourselves that prayer is an essential ingredient for fellowship with God in our quiet times.

So, what is a quiet time? It is not a religious ritual but an exciting opportunity. **It is a part of the day that we set aside for the worship of God, for the reading of the Word of God and for fellowship with God.**

Assessing the Need

Why have a Quiet Time?

It's your first week in a new job which you find stimulating and rewarding, and you're looking for some way to show your employer how enthusiastic you are about your work. The opportunity arises when your manager calls you into the office to find out how you're getting on. You tell her that you are enjoying the challenge and find the work interesting, but you would like to find out more about the background to the job. 'What do you mean?' she asks, with a bemused look. 'Well,' you reply, sensing that you haven't exactly made the impression you had intended, 'how does my work contribute to the final product that we put into the shops?' As you look across the desk you notice that she musters up a wry smile that thinly veils her impatience. 'Don't worry about that kind of thing', she says with a dismissive wave of the hand 'you just get on with your work.' And with those words, your manager signals the close of her interview by looking away from you and going back to the papers that litter the desk. You walk out of the office feeling belittled and sensing your enthusiasm ebbing away by the second.

If that has been your experience, you will have come to realise that it is much easier to perform a task, run an errand, or manage a project if you understand the thinking that lies behind it and the context in which it operates. That is why we're going to spend this chapter reflecting on the need for the quiet time and surveying the role that it plays in the Christian life.

First thing first

Jesus said the most important of all the commandments is to 'love the LORD your God with all your heart, with all your soul and with all your mind' (Matthew 22:37). And this must be our starting point.

In the course of writing this book, I have had the opportunity to speak to many people about the hurdles they have found difficult to overcome. One of the problems most frequently cited is that the pressures and demands of modern life make it extremely difficult to find time to be alone with God. People are under huge pressures in these days. Jobs are more demanding and less secure, hours are longer, and employers have high expectations of us; life seems to have accelerated to a hectic pace. Although this is a very real problem, we must remember that the Bible commands us to love the Lord our God with our entire mind, soul, and strength. If we are going to put that command into practice, we shouldn't allow these pressures to deprive us of our time with God. We need to take some counteractive measures.

We can begin our fight-back in the knowledge that we don't need to shoulder these pressures on our own. The New Testament tells us 'we do not have a High Priest who cannot sympathize with our weaknesses' (Hebrews 4:15). Jesus, our 'High Priest', became a real man and in the years that He lived on this earth He faced unimaginable pressures. If you look through the Gospels, you will read of instances when He was besieged by crowds, expressed grief, and endured pain. The Bible says that Jesus 'ever lives to make intercession' for us (Hebrews 7:25), this means that He constantly pleads on our behalf. What a comforting thought! Understanding the pressures we are under, Jesus takes our frail prayers and presents them to the Father.

When we have begun our 'fight back' in the knowledge that the Lord Jesus intercedes for us, we can draw on the relationship that we have with other members of God's family. The New Testament tells us we are 'members of … one body' (1 Corinthians 12:12) commanding us to 'bear one another's burdens' (Galatians 6:2). We need the help, prayer and support of other members of 'the household of faith' (Galatians 6:10), but we'll never benefit from this if we suffer in silence. Sharing our problems with other Christians helps them to understand the pressures that we have experienced, and their counsel will enable us to see things from a different perspective. Added to this will be the comfort of knowing that we have someone who will pray for us, encourage us and sometimes even gently reprove us.

Pressure of work and the pace of life do present a serious obstacle that can stand in the way of our quiet times, but there is a danger that we can use them as excuses. The Bible tells us 'the heart is deceitful above all things' (Jeremiah 17:9) and the claim that 'we can't find the time' might be masking the fact that we are not managing it properly. We can determine whether this is the case by making an audit of our lifestyle. This will be a simple matter of assessing the amount of time we spend sleeping, working, watching television, and whatever else we might be doing and comparing each result with the amount of time we spend alone with God. We can use this information to determine whether the problem can be eased by cutting down on watching television or pursuing a particular hobby that consumes a lot of our time, but be warned, it might be costly. We have all met people who say they are far too busy to get involved in the Lord's work, but always seem to find time for the things they really want to do. If we really love the Lord with our entire heart, soul, and strength, we will be prepared to make sacrifices so that we can spend time with Him.

Every Sunday morning I look through my sermon notes and spend time praying for the people who will be at the services to be held in my Church. I begin by praying that, rather than sleep in, they will use their time to come before God and prepare themselves to worship Him during the services. In the Ten Commandments, we are told that 'the seventh day is the Sabbath of the LORD your God' (Exodus 20:10), and whilst it provides us with an opportunity to take physical rest, its main purpose is to give us spiritual refreshment. Sundays provide us with a great opportunity to have a more 'in depth' quiet time without the pressures of the working day intruding into our minds, and we should use it to its full advantage.

Growing in our relationship

Although it was over twenty years ago, I can still remember the day I became a Christian, every part of my life seemed to bask in the light of my new relationship with God. I had been attending Church since I was a child, but on the day that I came to Christ, I discovered that Christianity is not a religion but a living relationship with God. In the days, weeks and months that followed I found that my quiet times were the nerve centre of that relationship.

One of the responsibilities of being a Pastor is to prepare people for marriage, and when I do so I always tell the 'happy couple' to make sure that their relationship develops. Sadly, there are times when married couples can be so caught up with their careers or busy with their Christian work that they don't invest the necessary time to grow together, and as a consequence their relationship suffers. In the same way, our relationship with God needs to develop, and the quiet time provides the fertile ground in which that growth will take place.

Communication channels

We live in the age of communication. We can pick up the telephone, send off a fax, or spin off e-mail with incredible ease. The technological revolution has shrunk our world into a 'global village.' However, while it is much easier to get in touch with one another we seem to be losing the most natural and effective form of communication—conversation! Communication involves more than an exchange of information, it encompasses interaction with other people, listening to their concerns and relaying our own. Whatever technological advances lie in wait for us in the years to come, nothing can replace this God given ability to relate to one another.

The ease with which modern technology facilitates communication might not stop with the effects that it has on the art of conversation; it can also affect the way that we approach God. There is a danger that we expect communication with Him to be as quick and as time effective as the way in which the technological revolution has made communication with one another. The result of this kind of thinking is that, instead of investing quality time with God, we rush off a spiritual 'e-mail' to Him—a quick prayer that provides a brief sketch of our needs. The prophet Isaiah once brought a serious charge against God's people which has a very important application to us: 'You turn things upside down' he said, 'as if the potter were thought to be like the clay!' (Isaiah 29:16). Why should God be expected to come to us on our terms, why should He send us a quick 'e-mail' so that it doesn't disturb our day too much? We have turned God's ways upside down; the Bible tells us that we are to wait upon God.

Head and heart

Have you ever met someone who has a phenomenal knowledge of the Bible but a distinct lack of grace in their life? They can reel off a string of verses they have memorised and can explain any Biblical doctrine you ask them about, but their life doesn't seem to match up to it. The reason for this may be that the Word of God is in their head but not in their hearts. Moses told the Israelites that 'the word is very near you: it is in your mouth and in your heart so that you may obey it' (Deuteronomy 30:14), and Jesus spoke about His Word abiding in us (John 15:7). The quiet time provides the opportunity for the Word to penetrate our hearts and transform our lives.

Discipleship

Before Jesus ascended into heaven, He said 'All authority has been given to Me in heaven and on earth. Go therefore and make disciples of all the nations' (Matthew 28:18-19). 'Disciple' comes from a Greek word having its origins in a verb, which means 'to learn'. The basic meaning of the word is a 'pupil' or a 'learner', so it is not surprising that Jesus went on to say that disciples must be taught everything that He has commanded (Matthew 28:20). Jewish teachers (Rabbis) had disciples who studied with them in the context of a very well defined relationship. A disciple would leave his own home, lodge with his teacher, and put himself under his authority. His purpose in life was to soak up his master's teaching and to follow his example.

Jesus gave the command to 'make disciples of all the nations' because discipleship is the normal pattern for the Christian life. Every Christian is a disciple, and like the pupils of those Rabbis, we need to soak up our Master's teaching, follow His example, and place ourselves under His authority. The quiet time is an important part of this process because it has been set aside in order to meet with God, learn from Him, and receive His Word.

Battle stations!

I once helped to lead a Christian holiday that involved an activity, which the brochure described as 'shooting the rapids.' This called for each of us to squeeze into a wet suit, grab a paddle, climb into a rubber raft and try to keep it on course as the river pulled us towards our destination. We didn't need to worry about the motion of the boat (the sheer force of the river saw to that) but we did need to work very hard to keep it on course as the current pulled us towards the edge of the river.

The Christian life can be a bit like 'shooting the rapids'; unless we take evasive action, we can be knocked off course by trials and temptations. We were born for battle; each day holds out the prospect of fresh conflict with the world, the flesh and the Devil, but the quiet time will equip us to fight these battles, overcome our enemy and keep on course. Jesus said 'in the world you will have tribulation; but be of good cheer, I have overcome the world.' (John 16:33) and John tells us that we are strong and that we 'overcome the wicked one' (Satan) when the Word of God abides in us (1 John 2:14).

Keeping clean

Whenever I eat in a café or restaurant I often look at the certificates that the owner displays, and in recent years I've noticed that the certificate of hygiene seems to have been given the top spot. This is not surprising, because as new viruses have emerged, public hygiene has become a very emotive issue, especially when it involves the preparation of food. In our home it has spurred us to ensure that, when working in the kitchen, we keep our hands clean at all times. Cleanliness is important for our spiritual health too, although in this case it is not our hands that we need to keep clean, but our heart. David asked 'who may ascend into the hill of the Lord?' then answering his question by saying 'he who has clean hands and a pure heart' (Psalm 24:3-4). In John's Gospel, Jesus tells us that the Word plays an important role in this process, saying: 'You are already clean because of the word which I have spoken to you' (John 15.3). And in Ephesians Paul talks about the way Christ cleanses us with 'the washing of water by the word' (Ephesians 5:26). This describes the way in which the Holy Spirit speaks through the Word showing us where we have sinned so that we can repent and be cleansed from the polluting effect that it has on our lives; but this can only happen if we spend time in God's Word.

Ponder the privilege

Peter tells us that 'angels long to look into the things that God has revealed to us' (1 Peter 1:12, NIV). Isn't it tragic that where angels long to look we can't always be bothered to glance! Perhaps we have begun to take God's blessings for granted. If you come to your quiet times feeling weary and wanting to get them over as quickly as possible, stop and think about the privilege that you have been given! You are able to meet with your Creator, you are invited to encounter Almighty God, to hear from Him and worship Him. What better reason could there possibly be to set the necessary time aside?

Gathering the Equipment

Every summer a warning is issued to people travelling to the National Parks. Hikers and climbers are asked to prepare for their journeys by keeping a watchful eye on the weather forecast and by making sure they are properly equipped. This is because there have been so many over-zealous people who have not bothered to listen to the forecast, and have set off with the wrong type of footwear. As a result, they have put themselves in great danger.

I hope that we have enthusiasm for our great venture; after all, what can possibly compete with the prospect of spending time with God? However, before we grab our Bible and head for our 'quiet corner', let's make sure that we are properly equipped.

Adopting the right attitude
At one of the regular times in which my Church Officers and I met for prayer, I told them I was planning my next series of sermons, but I was torn between two particular books, one of which was James. I asked them to pray that I would know which book to preach from. I didn't need to wait for an answer; a surge of enthusiasm seemed to reverberate around the room as every one of them told me to preach on James!

I imagine that their enthusiasm is a reliable index to the fervour that most Christians have for the book of James. People love it for its down to earth dynamism, and its practical teaching. We are going to spend the first part of this chapter in James, because he tells us everything we need to know about the spiritual preparation needed for the quiet time.

Let's start at the very end!
A famous sculptor was busily chipping away at a block of marble, when he sensed that he was being watched. Eventually the sound of the hammer hitting the chisel and the fragments of stone falling to the floor stopped as he looked down to see a very inquisitive young man who had been carefully watching every blow of his hammer. 'Can I help you young man?' said the artist. At this the spectator's face lit up; 'Yes you can!' he

said, with a note of excitement in his voice; 'Can you answer my question?' 'Well', said the sculptor, not wanting to be taken from his work, 'I'll do my best, but I am very busy; what is it?' 'How are you able to turn a block of marble into a beautiful statue?' There was a moment's silence, and then the artist smiled and said: 'It's quite simple really. I don't see the marble, I see a statue.'

That sculptor was able to turn a block of marble into a beautiful work of art because he never let the final objective leave his mind. The material we work with is far more precious, and like that artist, we should keep our eyes on the end result, which, according to James is 'the righteous life that God desires' (James 1:20 NIV). To achieve this goal we must be 'swift to hear, slow to speak, slow to wrath' (James 1:19), avoiding 'man's anger' which will prevent us from living 'the righteous life that God requires.' Having done these things we 'lay aside all filthiness and overflow of wickedness' so that we can be in the position to 'receive with meekness the implanted Word' (James 1:21).

Reaching our destination

Having told us about the end result, James tells us about three things that will help us to reach it.

A listening ear

A few years ago, I attended a conference at the Central Hall, Westminster, and during the lunch break my friend and I decided to walk to College Green, which was nearby. Although the name wasn't familiar to me, I instantly recognised it because it is used by the media to interview politicians, and it is seen on our television screens almost every night. It happened to be a time of crisis for the British Government, and the Green seemed to be swarming with reporters, cameramen, and members of the public. I found it fascinating to watch the effect that the arrival of a Member of Parliament had upon the journalists. They dropped whatever they were doing, rushed over to him, asked all sorts of questions, and made a careful note of every word that he spoke. James tells us that, like those reporters, we need to be 'swift to hear'. If we are 'swift to hear' God's Word, we will be ready to receive what He tells us, and to put it into practice. This will involve grasping every opportunity to learn about God's Word, and aiming to grow in our understanding of it.

A good test of whether we have 'listening ears' would be to ask ourselves what we do when the going gets tough. Do we get so consumed with our problems that we put God's Word aside, and devote our quiet times to praying that we will escape the difficulties that have hit us? Or do we ask God for wisdom, and search the scriptures to see how we can glorify Him in the situation in which we find ourselves? In the opening verses of this chapter, James addresses the issue of trials. He tells us to 'count it all joy' when they arrive because they are God's tool to test our faith and develop patience, which will result in spiritual maturity (see James 1:2-4 NIV). James' readers seem to have been shaken by the trials that had been unleashed on them. They appear to have failed to see their difficulties in the context of the work that God was doing in their lives, and they had forfeited the divine wisdom that was available to them. This kind of wisdom is described by John Blanchard as 'the God given insight into our human circumstances and situations that enables a man to see God's will, coupled with a whole-hearted desire to see it done.'[4] The result of their neglect seems to have been disastrous; a lack of wisdom left them totally unprepared for their trials, and because of this they yielded to temptation, fell into sin, and they had become dull to God's Word. The connection between God's Word and their hearts had come loose, how should they tighten it? They had to get back to the Word, so that they could return to a spiritual understanding of their problems.

Reluctant tongues

In contrast to this readiness to listen to God's Word, James tells us that we should be 'slow to speak' (James 1:19). Human nature takes us in the opposite direction; our instinct tells us that we must have our own say before anyone else gets a chance. God turns that process upside down! We should be quick to listen to what He has to say, and slow to speak on our own behalf. These three words, 'slow to speak', are bursting with potential application, but the context is all about receiving God's Word in order that we might gain wisdom, resist temptation and live 'the righteous life that God requires.' What kind of speech is James talking about? He is probably thinking of all kinds of rash words but, in view of the fact that he goes on to tell us to 'be slow to wrath', it would seem that his emphasis is upon words that are spoken in anger. Our own shortcomings will confirm that angry words, spoken in the heat of the moment, sour our spiritual lives and stifle the Word of God.

Uncluttered lives

Having told us to be 'swift to hear, slow to speak, slow to wrath', James turns the spotlight onto our lives. 'Therefore, lay aside all filthiness and overflow of wickedness.' (James 1:21). The word 'lay aside' was used to describe the way that you would peel off filthy or stained clothes, it was also used to talk about moral evil, and its root word would sometimes be used to describe ear wax. What a powerful picture! In the same way that wax can dull our hearing, sin will diminish our ability to listen to the Word of God. We must ensure that our lives are uncluttered by sin through self-examination, confession of sin, and repentance.

The right reception

After telling us to be 'swift to hear' (James 1:19), James urges us to 'receive with meekness the implanted Word, which is able to save (our) souls' (James 1:21).

Perhaps you have stumbled across this particular verse before and broken out in a cold sweat; 'what does he mean when he says "the word is able to save your souls"?' You may have asked yourself, 'does it mean that my salvation might be in question?' The last thing that James would want to do would be to make us doubt our salvation, far from it – he wants us to be more confident about it. The problem lies with our tendency to see salvation as something that happened in the past, (the day that we came to Christ) while the New Testament presents it as something that embraces past, present and future. We were saved from the guilt and the penalty of sin on the day that we turned from our sin (repented) and trusted in Christ. We continue to be saved from the power of sin by the presence of the Holy Spirit in our lives. And on the great day that lies ahead of us, we will stand before the Judgement Seat and be saved from the wrath of God. These three dimensions are brought together in the work that God is doing through His

Word. The Word of God brought us to Christ, acts as a catalyst for our growth in Christ, and promises us a 'not guilty' verdict on Judgement Day.

The agricultural picture that James uses in these verses bears a resemblance to the parable of the sower. Our hearts are the soil, from which we must weed out anger and sin, and God's Word is the seed that has been 'implanted' in our hearts. The fact that it has been 'implanted' does not mean that we need only receive it once, it means that the Word becomes 'a permanent, inseparable part'[5] of us. And if this is going to happen we must feed on God's Word on a day-by-day basis. The word 'receive' means that we welcome the Word without resistance or adverse reaction, and this will involve accepting it 'with meekness'; 'a humble and gentle attitude, which expresses itself in a patient submissiveness'.[6]

Living the Word

Before I went into the ministry, my employers sent me on a course in Business Management. One of my projects required me to produce a training programme for school leavers starting a new job. I toiled over an empty piece of paper for hours, until I finally produced something that I felt was balanced, effective, and interesting. When I got the work back from my tutor, he told me my programme needed 'more hands-on experience.' This was another way of saying that whilst theory is important, practice is essential, and if we look at the next few verses we'll see James say something very similar.

'But be doers of the word, and not hearers only, deceiving yourselves. For if anyone is a hearer of the word and not a doer, he is like a man observing his natural face in a mirror; for he observes himself, goes away, and immediately forgets what kind of man he was. But he who looks into the perfect law of liberty and continues in it, and is not a forgetful hearer but a doer of the work, this one will be blessed in what he does.' (James 1:22-25).

James is very concerned that we put God's Word into practice, and to get his point across he gives us two illustrations. First, he describes a man who looks at himself in a mirror and does nothing about what he sees. This sounds a little like me on a Sunday morning; it's a good thing that my congregation can't see what goes on in my vestry just before the service begins. My Deacons often have to remind me that my hair is sticking up or my tie isn't straight. This is because I have been like the man that James describes. I have glanced at the mirror, noticed that my tie isn't straight or that my hair seems to have developed a life of its own, but I have been so pre-occupied with thoughts about the service that I have forgotten to do anything about it. In the same way in which the man in James' illustration takes the time to look at himself in the mirror and fails to make any necessary adjustments, we can take the time to look into the Word but neglect to put it into practice.

The second illustration provided by James, paints the picture of a man who 'looks into the perfect law of liberty and continues in it' (James 1:25). 'The perfect law of liberty' is a very striking description of the Word of God; it is 'law' because it sets God's standards, it is 'perfect' because it has been fulfilled and made complete by Christ, and it brings 'liberty' because it has been written on our hearts (Jeremiah 31:33). James is telling us that there is nothing superficial about the way that this man handles the Word. The phrase 'looks intently' describes the way that you might stop and bend down to make a very careful, precise examination of something.

Which man are you most like? If you are more like the man who looks in the mirror and goes away, don't despair! Honesty is half the battle, and having faced up to this you have taken your first step towards changing. There may not be as huge a gap between the two men as you might think; the first man takes the time and the effort to hear the Word of God, but his short-coming is that he doesn't put it into practice. It's a matter of doing as well as hearing.

How can you make sure that you hear God's Word and put it into practice? During your next quiet time write down the verse that has challenged you the most and ask God to show you how you can put it into practice. Don't leave it within the confines of your quiet time—bring the verse to mind during the day. When I was still living with my parents, my father used to drive me to college. One morning I had memorised Philippians 2:3: 'let nothing be done through selfish ambition or conceit, but in lowliness of mind let each esteem others better than himself'. That morning my father was running a little late, and I was about to express my impatience when I brought the verse to mind, and decided to exercise a little patience! Another benefit of making a note of the verse which has challenged you is that you can review it the next day. And if it hasn't sunk in, it might be wiser to stick with it for another day, so you can be sure it has become part of your life. Include it in your prayers too. I have a notebook that I fill with prayer needs, and some of the pages contain lists of scriptures with very brief comments. Recently, through my study of Colossians, the Lord has spoken to me about my ministry, and in the page of my notebook marked 'ministry' I have written the reference Colossians 2:2. Consequently whenever I pray about this area, I turn to that verse, and pray that my ministry might bring encouragement to people so that they will be 'knit together in love, and attaining to all riches of the full assurance of understanding.'

Tools for the job

Now that we have examined our attitude towards the Word of God and thought about the way in which we should receive it, we can move on to inspect our 'tool kit.'

A reliable Commentary

The great American preacher and writer, A W Tozer once said 'it is a dangerous and costly practice to consult men every time we reach a dark spot in the scriptures ... a few minutes of earnest prayer will give more light than hours of reading the commentaries. The best rule is: Go to God first about the meaning of any text. Then consult the teachers, they may have found a grain of wheat that you overlooked.'[7] This is an important note of caution. A commentary is a very useful tool if we are unsure about the meaning of a passage – but we mustn't let it do our thinking for us.

Which Commentary?

If you only have the funds for one volume, the best modern commentary available is the 'New Bible Commentary'[8]. However, if you want some solid historical literature Matthew Henry's Commentary is available in a condensed volume. Although written in the seventeenth century, his work is very understandable. He is easy to read, clear in his interpretation and handles the text with the greatest of skill. The 'Tyndale Commentaries'[9] provide a concise, scholarly treatment of many New and Old Testament books, whilst the 'Welwyn Series'[10] has a more practical emphasis. If you are looking for a more in-depth treatment of the Scripture you will find 'The Bible Speaks Today'[11] series ideal, and if you want to dig a little deeper without getting weighed down by academic argument William Hendriksen's 'New Testament Commentaries'[12] are very beneficial.

This list is not exhaustive. If you want to look into it more read Don Carson's 'New Testament Commentary Survey'[13] and Tremper Longman III's 'Old Testament Commentary Survey'[14].

A Concordance

What's the verse that is on the tip of your tongue, and how can you track it down? This is where a concordance is useful. Most Study Bibles include one, but their scope will be very limited, and if you want to engage in some serious Bible study, you will need a more comprehensive volume. For those looking for a concordance that covers the majority of the words in the Bible, 'Strong's Exhaustive Concordance' or 'Young's Analytical Concordance' can be used in conjunction with the King James Version, and the 'NIV Exhaustive Concordance' with the New International Version. Whilst such detailed concordances can be very helpful, 'Cruden's Concordance of the Bible', a more concise volume, will give you all that you need. If you have a personal computer, it would be well worth investing in a good Bible programme that will enable you to search for any verse in the Bible at high speed.

A notebook

The writer to the Hebrews tells us that 'we must give the more earnest heed to the things we have heard, lest we drift away' (Hebrews 2:1), and if we are serious about committing something to memory, we'll make a note of it.

People!

'Support groups' have become very popular in our society, but the idea isn't particularly new – it's in the Bible. The New Testament encourages us to 'consider one another in order to stir up love and good works' (Hebrews 10:24). True, the quiet time is by definition a solitary exercise, but we need the encouragement and support of one another. If you are having problems with your quiet times, how about forming a 'support group' with other people who struggle? Think of the benefit of such an exercise. You could pray for one another, pass on encouragement, share practical ideas, pool your insights into particular books of the Bible, and help each other when you go through difficult patches in your devotional lives.

Nuts and bolts

You've got up early, found a quiet corner, opened your Bible and you're full of enthusiasm, but there's one awkward question wriggling away at the back of your mind—what do you do next? Although we might regard the quiet time as an important part of our Christian life, many of us are not certain about how we should best use it. The typical questions I have been asked are 'what parts of the Bible should I read? How long should my quiet time be? What proportion of the time should I spend praying? What should I be praying about?'

In the course of this chapter we'll address those questions and concentrate on practicalities so that we can make the most of our quiet times.

Charting the course

Passengers in my car often ask me if I know where I'm going, and this is because I have a poor sense of direction, which often takes me on time-consuming detours. If we are going to get the most from the time that we set aside to be alone with God, a sense of direction is essential, so before we go any further we'll spend a little time charting the course.

The most effective navigational tool at hand is a simple exercise. Turn the clock forward, imagine we have closed our Bibles, said our 'amen' and we are about to launch into the activities of the day. What should have been going on in the intervening time and what difference will it have made?

We will have encountered God

If it were not for God's promises, it might seem a little presumptuous to take this for granted. God's promises are very different from those that you or I might announce. We make promises for all sorts of reasons; we might make a promise that we genuinely intend to keep, or we may just be going through the motions in order to placate someone. God's promises however announce His intentions and reveal His nature. Michael Horton, an American Pastor, puts it beautifully when he says that 'God has minted His will into the coins of promises, and apart from the coinage of the realm, we cannot know God's mind or heart.'[15]

God announced His plan that Abraham's offspring would include people like us—those who have become part of the family of God through Christ—when He promised that Abraham would become 'a father of many nations' (Genesis 17:4). The New Testament establishes the means of forgiveness of sin when it promises that if we confess our sins God will forgive us, and cleanse us (1 John 1:9). James provides us with the basis of our expectation to meet with God when he promises that if we 'draw near to God' He will 'draw near' to us (James 4:8). And Hebrews tells us we can have 'boldness to enter the Holiest by the blood of Jesus, by a new and living way which He consecrated for us' (Hebrews 10:19-20). This is why our expectation to meet with God is not a presumption; it is a matter of taking God at His Word.

Although we can be confident that we will encounter God, we mustn't use our feelings as a gauge to determine whether this has taken place. Sometimes we will come away feeling joyful and satisfied but at other times, we might feel unhappy and frustrated. When we find ourselves experiencing the latter rather than the former we must remember that it is we who have changed, not God, and it is not an indication that the Lord has forsaken us.

While God's Word gives us grounds to be confident that we will meet with Him, we mustn't forget that the Bible warns us that sin and rebellion will grieve the Holy Spirit and deprive us of this privilege. The Psalmist said 'if I regard iniquity in my heart, the Lord will not hear' (Psalm 66:18). The New Testament warns us against 'the deceitfulness of sin' (Hebrews 3:13), so it is important to ask the Holy Spirit to search our hearts and show us whether there is any sin we have not confessed to God. David's prayer was 'search me, O God, and know my heart; try me, and know my anxieties; and see if there is any wicked way in me, and lead me in the way everlasting' (Psalm 139:23-24). While this helps us to keep short accounts with God, we needn't spend too much time agonizing over it, because we can be certain that if there is sin to be dealt with, God will convict us of it.

What happens when we have an encounter with God? We have to be careful not to force God's ways into neatly arranged categories, but we can identify a number of things the Bible associates with our meeting God.

First, we will be aware of God's presence. For the people of Israel wandering through the wilderness this was something visible; it was the cloud that led them by day and the pillar of fire by night (Exodus 13:21). It was also seen in the cloud of glory that descended to the Tabernacle and latterly in the Temple (Exodus 33:9, 2 Chronicles 7:1). In the New Testament this awareness moves from the visible to the invisible, God makes us aware of His presence through the work of the Holy Sprit because 'we have access to the Father by one Spirit' (Ephesians 2:18 NIV).

Secondly, we will have a conviction, or an assurance, that we are part of God's family. This is what Paul is talking about when He says 'because you are sons, God sent the Spirit of his Son into our hearts, the Spirit who calls out, 'Abba', Father' (Galatians 4:6). The word 'Abba' comes from the language that Jesus would have spoken; it is the Aramaic word for 'father' that was reserved for informality and intimacy. Jesus used this word to address His Father and now that God has sent His Holy Spirit into our hearts we can relate to Him in the same way.

Thirdly, we will experience spiritual blessing. Like the word 'fellowship', that we thought about in chapter one, 'blessing' can be put to many uses in our modern vocabulary, but it is important to understand what the Bible means when it uses the word. There are two words in the New Testament which translate as 'bless' and 'blessing'. One is **makarios,** which means 'happy' or 'favoured.' This word is used by Jesus to describe a happiness that is dependent upon God and detached from the things of this world (Matthew 5:2-12). The other is **eulogia**, which means 'to speak well of'; this can be used to speak about God and man. When it is used to speak about God it is connected with worship (1 Peter 1:3 NKJ) and when it is used to speak about man it describes the 'good gifts that God bestows'[16].

In the Old Testament 'blessing' was largely used to describe the material benefits that God gave to His people (Deuteronomy 28:1-14, Genesis 26:12-13). However, the New Testament concept of blessing focuses on the spiritual things that God has given to the children of the New Covenant. Paul opens his letter to the Ephesians underlining this by saying 'blessed be the God and Father of our Lord Jesus Christ, who has blessed us with every spiritual blessing in the heavenly places in Christ,' (Ephesians 1:3). 'Spiritual' makes a distinction from the material blessings that had played such an important part in the life of the Old Testament people of God.

'Heavenly' locates these blessings in 'the unseen world of spiritual reality'[17] and 'in Christ' shows us that we receive them through the Lord Jesus. Since Paul specifies that nothing has been withheld from us, in saying we have been blessed 'with every spiritual blessing', we can come to our quiet times in the knowledge that God will not be frugal with His blessing.

We will have heard God's voice

Doubtless, you have met people who claim to have heard God speak. Some might have gone so far as to say that they hear an audible voice, others may describe it as an experience, which takes place within the confines of their mind, but most of them have misunderstood the way that God communicates with us. When the New Testament writers talk about hearing God (Romans 10:17), they are not describing the way that we might listen to an audible voice or some kind of inspired thought, they are talking about the way we receive the Word of God. When Jesus explained the meaning of the parable of the sower, He related every scene that He had presented to the way in which the Word had been received. For example, the meaning that lay behind the birds of the air that had seized the seed relates to instances of people who hear the 'word of the kingdom' without understanding it (Matthew 13:19). Paul writes to the Christians in Rome, forging a link between hearing from God and the preaching of the Word, asking 'how then shall they call on Him in whom they have not believed? And how shall they believe in Him of whom they have not heard? And how shall they hear without a preacher?' (Romans 10:14). And in the very first few verses of the book of Revelation John says 'blessed is he who reads and those who hear the words of this prophecy, and keep those things which are written in it; for the time is near' (Revelation 1:3).

In order to grasp this we will need to look at the way in which God has communicated with His people through the different stages of His plan.

In the Old Testament, Abraham and Jacob heard directly from God, although He often spoke to them through visions. At the beginning of the chapter setting out God's covenant with Abraham we are told the Word of the LORD came to Abram in a vision' (Genesis 15.1). When Jacob had a vision of a ladder that rested on earth and reached up to heaven (Genesis 28:10-22) God told him that he and his descendants would be given the land upon which he lay.

Although there are instances in the Old Testament where people receive a Word directly from God, for much of the time God chose to communicate His Word through the prophets. Amos tells us that 'the Lord God does nothing, unless He reveals His secret to His servants the prophets' (Amos 3:7), in Hosea God tells us that He has 'spoken by the prophets' (Hosea 12:10). And Peter tells us that the Old Testament prophets were able to speak about the sufferings of Christ because of 'the Spirit of Christ who was in them' (1 Peter 1:11).

At the end of Jesus' earthly ministry He told the disciples that He would be leaving this world, promising to send the Holy Spirit.

'When He, the Spirit of truth, has come, He will guide you into all truth; for He will not speak on His own authority, but whatever He hears He will speak; and He will tell you things to come. He will glorify Me, for He will take of what is Mine and declare it to you. All things that the Father has are Mine. Therefore I said that He will take of Mine and declare it to you.' (John 16:13-15)

In the light of these statements it is not surprising that when John speaks on behalf of his fellow apostles he says: 'We are of God. He who knows God hears us; he who is not of God does not hear us. By this we know the spirit of truth and the spirit of error' (1 John 4:6). Peter speaks in a similar way when he writes about Paul's letters and 'the rest of the Scriptures' in the same stroke of a pen (2 Peter 3:16). Jesus had fulfilled His promise that the Holy Spirit would lead the apostles into 'all truth', and the truth of which He spoke is the New Testament.

This leaves us with the Bible; and every time we open it, we should stop and consider what we hold in our hand. The Bible is God's Word, and we read it, meditate on it, and treasure it because it is His means of communication with us.

LAYING THE FOUNDATION—The time, The place

My father is an irrepressible morning person. My childhood memories are littered with images of him bouncing out of his bedroom each morning, singing in the shower and leaving the house with the maximum amount of noise that he could possibly muster. Much to my wife's distress, I am very similar and consequently I find early morning the best part of the day to devote to my quiet time. Whether you are a 'morning person' or not I would encourage you to do the same. It provides a good start, it gives you something to take into the day, and it focuses your mind on the Lord before you throw yourself into the activities that lie ahead of you. However, there is no hard and fast rule about this, you might feel more comfortable with a period in the middle of the day, in the evening, or at the end of the day. The important thing is that you have a regular time, which becomes part of the pattern of your life.

If you want to find the right place for your quiet time you only need to ask yourself one simple question: 'where can I be free from distractions?' It could be the kitchen, the lounge, the shed, the car, or a bench in the park. It doesn't really matter as long as you can be sure that you will be left alone.

How long?

Have you ever been inspired by the biography of a great man of God, such as John Wesley, George Whitefield, or A W Tozer—a man who unflinchingly got himself out of bed each morning and spent hour after hour in the presence of God? If you are anything like me you would have closed the book, vowed to follow his example, tried it the next morning and failed miserably! I have come to learn that the problem centres on a misconception; the idea that if I spend the same amount of time the man of whom I have read spent in prayer, I could be as much a man of God as he. The flaw in this idea is that I have failed to realise that, unlike me, he didn't keep his eye on the clock because he was taken up with God, and time was the last thing on his mind. It is not important that we spend twenty minutes, half an hour or even an hour engaged in our quiet time, what matters is that we meet with God. We should just be sure to set aside enough time so that we don't need to rush.

What parts of the Bible should we read?

If the Bible is God's Word, we should not consider one part of it to be more or less the Word of God than another. Consequently, we don't need to get concerned about which particular book we should be reading. If we use our common sense and follow a useful Bible reading plan, God will use the passages of Scripture that we read each day for 'teaching, rebuking, correcting' and for 'training in righteousness' (2 Timothy 3:16, NIV).

I have become alarmed at the way in which the Old Testament is neglected, and increasingly convinced of the need for a balanced diet of Old and New Testaments. The most effective way to do this is to follow a reading plan that takes you through the whole of the Bible in a year or two. A two-year Bible reading plan is provided in the appendix of this book.

Constructing a framework

Now that we have laid the foundation for the quiet time, we can begin to construct a framework. However, we do need to sound a note of caution; human beings have a tendency to turn a liberating principle into something that is inflexible and legalistic, so we must make sure that our framework is a flexible guide rather than a binding law.

From the moment we wake up to the second we drift into sleep, there are all sorts of thoughts swimming around in our minds demanding that we give them our undivided attention. Unfortunately, they do not vanish in the time that we have set aside to meet with God, but we will be able to put them to one side if we take a few minutes to harness our thoughts and channel them in the right direction. I have found Hallesby's classic book on prayer very helpful in this matter. His advice is; 'take plenty of time before you speak. Let quietude wield its influence upon you. Let the fact that you are alone assert itself. Give your soul time to get released from the many outward things…. Let the devotional attitude, the attitude of holy passivity, open all the doors of the soul leading into the realm of eternal things.'[18] In addition to this, it is helpful to read a few pages of a devotional book. There are many such books available. The most inspiring I have used is 'Renewed day by Day'[19] which is a selection of the writings of A.W.Tozer divided into daily portions. One of the reasons this is such a valuable book is that Tozer treasured the quiet time and enjoyed an intensely close relationship with God and this radiates from his writing. Other books which have the same kind of value are J.C. Ryle's 'Expository thoughts on the Gospels' [20], C.H Spurgeon's 'Morning and Evening'[21] and 'Drawing near' by John MacArthur[22]. One word of warning—no matter how helpful these books might be, we mustn't forget they have been written by men while the Bible has been inspired by God. Consequently, we should be careful to spend the bulk of our time in the Word of God. The purpose of using a devotional book, however valuable, is to get the brain into the right gear and the heart into the right place.

Once we have put our minds into the right gear, we should move on to praise. Without laying down hard and fast rules let me provide a few principles that I have found to be helpful in this area.

Turn the verses that encouraged you yesterday into today's praise. For example, one morning the Lord spoke to me through Psalm 84:10; 'a day in Your courts is better than a thousand.' The courts that the Psalmist speaks of are the courts of the temple, but in the New Covenant, we can understand this to speak of the way in which we are able to continually remain in the presence of God. The next morning this verse served as the basis for my worship. I praised God for the way that He has enabled me to dwell in His presence. I worshipped the Son of God who has shed His blood so that I might enjoy this privilege, and I rejoiced in the fact that God welcomes me into His presence as a Father welcomes His son.

Whether you have the voice of gold or gravel, spend a few moments worshipping the Lord in song. Keep a songbook with you, and look for something that might have a particular link with the theme you have chosen for the focus of your praise. The additional benefit will be that the songs that you choose will become more meaningful when you next sing them in Church.

Our Christian Bookshops seem to be bursting at the seams with 'worship resources' but the best resource we have to hand is the Bible. I trained for the ministry at an Anglican Theological College and one of the things I found very helpful about their daily act of worship was the way in which a different psalm was read aloud by the whole congregation. Of course, there is no need to be confined to the psalms, the Bible is packed with songs of praise and words of worship which will enable us to worship God 'in spirit and truth' (John 4:24).

Get down to God's Word
The central part of the quiet time involves reading God's Word, and since it

is a unique and powerful book we need to be sure that we are 'rightly dividing the Word of truth' (2 Timothy 2:15). How do we do this? Here are four principles that will point us in the right direction.

First, we should read the passage intelligently. The Bible places a lot of emphasis on the importance of our minds. Jesus said that the greatest of all the Commandments is to 'love the LORD your God with all your heart, with all your soul, and with all your **mind**' (Matthew 22:37). And Paul told Timothy that 'God has not given us a spirit of fear, but of power and of love and of a sound **mind**.' (2 Timothy 1:7). With such an importance placed on our minds, we need to put them to work as we read the Word. Questions can be a very helpful part of this process. Here are some examples:

▶ How does this passage fit in with the one that I read in the last chapter?
▶ What is it all about?
▶ What does it tell me about the way that God's plan is unfolding?
▶ What does it tell me about God the Father, God the Son, and God the Holy Spirit?
▶ Is there anything I need to study further?
▶ Does any other passage of the Bible throw light on this?
▶ Does it expose a sin in my life?
▶ What is it challenging me to do?

Secondly, whilst it is important that we use our minds, we have to realise that we won't get very far without the illumination provided by the Holy Spirit. This is distinct from revelation; revelation is already provided within the pages of the Bible, but illumination enables us to understand it. Imagine that as dusk begins to fall a letter drops onto your doormat. You tear it open, you can just about read some of the words, and you know who it's from, but the lack of light prevents you from reading it all the way through. What will you do; ask for another message that you can understand? Of course not, you'll switch the light on! Whenever we come to God's Word, we need the Holy Spirit to provide the necessary 'light' so that we can understand what God is saying and receive it into our hearts and lives. That's what David is talking about when he says 'Open my eyes, that I may see wondrous things from Your law… Teach me, O LORD, the way of Your statutes, and I shall keep it to the end. Give me understanding, and I shall keep Your law; indeed, I shall observe it with my whole heart' (Psalm 119:18, 33-34).

When we come to the New Testament, we cannot do better than look at the way in which Jesus provided illumination for the disciples who were treading the road to Emmaus. They were confused, depressed, and disappointed. Luke tells us that when the Lord Jesus joined them 'their eyes were restrained' (Luke 24:16), so that they were kept from recognising Him. In the course of the conversation, they told him that their hopes that they might have found the Messiah had been shattered by Jesus' brutal execution on the cross. After they had poured out their hearts to the mystery traveller, they found themselves at the receiving end of a Bible study of breathtaking proportions; Jesus took them through the Old Testament and showed them that it taught that the Messiah must go to the cross. The disciple's mood suddenly changed from despair to joy because Jesus had 'opened their understanding that they might comprehend the Scriptures' (Luke 24:45). When they realised that the mystery traveller was Jesus, they said to one another 'Did not our heart burn within us while He talked with us on the road, and while He opened the Scriptures to us?' (Luke 24:32).

Thirdly, we will need to meditate on God's Word. Meditation seems to have been a regular feature in David's life 'I will meditate on your precepts and contemplate your ways' he declares (Psalm 119:15). 'Oh, how I love your law! It is my meditation all the day ' (Psalm 119:97). When Joshua stood on the verge of claiming the Promised Land he was told: 'This Book of the Law shall not depart from your mouth, but you shall meditate in it day and night, that you may observe to do according to all that is written in it. For then you will make your way prosperous, and then you will have good success' (Joshua 1:8). Psalm 1 declares: 'Blessed is the man who walks not in the counsel of the ungodly, nor stands in the path of sinners, nor sits in the seat of the scornful; but his delight is in the law of the LORD, And in His law he meditates day and night' (Psalm 1:1-2).

The word 'meditate' used in those passages describes the way in which someone might talk the Scriptures through, or read the words aloud. For example when David said 'I meditate on all your works. I muse on the work of your hands' (Psalm 143:5) he is describing the way in which he recounts God's works to himself. To borrow a phrase from Martyn Lloyd Jones, he is 'addressing himself in the Lord.'[23]

The second Old Testament word that speaks about meditation describes the way one might rehearse something and go over it in one's mind, and it is used to speak about silent or audible reflection of God's works. One of the Psalmists had been tossing and turning through the night, distress had robbed him of his sleep 'my hand was stretched out in the night without ceasing' he said 'my soul refused to be comforted' (Psalm 77:2). Look at the following verses and notice the way in which he alleviates his distress.

I call to remembrance my song in the night;
I meditate within my heart,
And my spirit makes diligent search.
Will the Lord cast off forever?
And will He be favourable no more?
… And I said, "This is my anguish;
But I will remember the years of the right hand of the Most High'
(Psalm 77:6-7,10).

There is just one reference to meditation in the New Testament which can be found in 1 Timothy 4:15: 'Meditate on these things; give yourself entirely to them, that your progress may be evident to all'. The meaning of the Greek word is to give careful attention, to show diligence, to study or to ponder.

If we put these Biblical words together, we will understand that when we meditate on God's Word we do more than merely read it. We will give careful attention to what we read, we will reflect on what it tells us about God the Father, Son and Holy Spirit, we will work the implications through and we will receive it into our hearts and lives.

Finally, we need to respond to the passage that we have read, in prayer. Many people treat prayer as a shopping list of needs that they want to bring to God. While there is a place for presenting requests to God, the first thing that we should do is to make sure that we are living in obedience to Him. I often use the 'ACTS' formula to do this. Using the passage that I have been reading I spend some time in **adoration**, I then **confess** the sin that I have been made aware of, I move on to **thanksgiving** and then I make my **supplications** (i.e. I bring specific prayer requests to God). This helps me ensure that the verses I have been reading become part of my life.

What about Bible notes?

You don't have to look very far to find a copy of some Bible notes. There seems to be a multitude in print and the fact that there is such a demand for them suggests that people find them helpful. Bible notes can be useful tools but they do have their limitations. The Bible is without error but Bible notes are not, so we must feel free to disagree with them or even discard them if they are no longer helpful. We should take great care that we do not read our notes more than we read the Bible; nor must we let them do our work for us. I become very concerned when I see Christians using notes providing a short verse and telling a little story which leads to a challenge, as their main spiritual meal of the day. We should regard Bible notes as a menu, they help us appreciate the meal, but they don't feed us. I treat them as a back-up, only using them if I have a bit of a 'block', and I encourage others to do the same. A lot of people have become so dependent upon Bible notes that they lose the wonderful experience of unearthing treasures from the Word of God for themselves. After all, when God fed His people with manna from heaven, they didn't need to follow a guidebook; they just went out and collected it. Try it, you'll have a great surprise in store!

What about your Pastor's sermons?

I don't get to hear too many sermons because I tend to be preaching them, but when I do I make the most of them. I take notes, I identify the central theme, I seize on the main challenge and then pray the issues through. James warns us not to be 'hearers only' but to put the Word into practice (James 1:22). How can we expect to do that if we don't use our quiet times to work through the challenge that our Pastor has brought to us from God's Word?

We have laid a foundation, constructed a framework, and thought about the practical issues. Now it's over to you to go out and explore the quiet time for yourself.

Extending the Territory

No matter how nutritious and well balanced your diet may be there are always times when you might welcome a change. In the last chapter, we thought about the 'nuts and bolts' of the quiet time, but we should be careful not to be so organised and methodical that we become stale. In this chapter, we are going to think about ways in which we can vary the quiet time, so that we can keep ourselves fresh. We are going to look at a day to day plan that will take us through a character study, a theme, a biblical prayer, and an overview of a book.

Peter: A Character Study

Peter describes Himself as 'an apostle of Jesus Christ' (1 Peter 1:1), an 'eyewitness of His (Christ's) majesty ', and 'a fellow elder' (1 Peter 5:1). We know that he was a spokesman for the disciples and a leading figure in the early Church (John 1:16, Acts 1:15-26). However, the Bible gives us an honest portrayal of this disciple, showing us his weaknesses as well as his strengths, and we can take heart from the way that the Lord uses Him, despite his failings.

Day 1: Peter the Disciple

Read Mark 1:16-17

These verses describes Peter's calling. Think about the immediacy of his response. Move on to Luke 5:1-11 and note the way that he responds to Jesus.

Read Mark 5:37, 9:2

Alongside James and John, Peter was particularly close to Jesus.
Think about Peter's relationship with Jesus and compare it to your own.

Prayer Pointers

▶ Thank the Lord for the way in which He has called you into a living relationship.

▶ Go back to Peter's response to Jesus in Luke 5:8; ask the Holy Spirit to give you a sense of Christ's presence, so that you will be conscious of your own sinfulness and resolved to live a holy life.

▶ Pray about your relationship with the Lord Jesus, and expect to get closer to Him.

Day 2: Peter the enthusiast

Peter is often criticised for his impulsive outbursts, but we must give him credit for his enthusiastic devotion to the

Lord, which is a great asset, if properly channelled. Peter's problem was not his enthusiasm itself; it lay in the fact that it was sporadic and unreliable.

Read Matthew 14:22-33

Think about Peter's readiness to do what the Lord asks of him. How does that compare to you?

Identify what went wrong. Are there instances in your life that bear a similarity? If so, think about what these verses teach you.

Look at the ways that Jesus saves Peter from sinking, compare this to David's words in Psalm 37:23-24. What encouragement can you draw from this?

Prayer Pointers

▶ Thank the Lord that He is always there to lift you when you fall, and to save you when you are sinking.

▶ Ask your Heavenly Father to show you the areas where your Christian life needs more balance and consistency. Read Hebrews 12:1-2 and prayerfully determine to keep your eyes on Jesus.

Day 3: Peter's denial of Jesus

Read Mark 14:27-31

Jesus warned Peter that he would deny Him. Compare Jesus' repeated warning with Peter's refusal to face them.

What do Peter's words in verse 29 tell

about his understanding of Jesus' words (verses 27-28)?

Think about the way that Peter's response in verse 31 leaves him vulnerable to the temptation to deny his Lord.

Read Mark's account of the denial (Mark 14:66-72), remembering that there are times that each of us denies the Lord.

Prayer Pointers

▶ Thank God for the way that He overrules your mistakes and uses them for His glory.

▶ Ask Him to show you the areas of vulnerability that you have not yet faced up to.

▶ Pray for anyone known to you who might feel that they have let the Lord down.

Day 4: The road to recovery

Read Mark 16:7

Think about the significance of this instruction in the light of Peter's denial of Jesus.

Read John 21:1-14 and look at the way in which Peter expressed joy at the sight of the risen Lord Jesus.

Read John 21:15-19, and then go back to concentrate on verse 15. What is Jesus calling Peter to do?

What did Jesus ask Peter in three

separate instances? Do you think that this has anything to say about what should motivate Peter?

Don't forget the cost that Peter had to be prepared to pay (18-19), have you counted the cost of putting the Lord first in your life?

Prayer Pointers

❱ Praise God that He loves and forgives you. Thank Him for the privilege of being one of His 'lambs.'

❱ Confess any false motives that you might have, and ask God to help you to be motivated by love.

❱ Pray that you would be ready to follow the Lord, at any cost, and care for His people at all times.

Day 5: Peter the preacher (1)

In Acts 2 we meet a very different Peter from the person who denied his Lord. Read the chapter through, looking for the source of this transformation.

Look at verses 17-21 where Peter identifies a passage from the prophet Joel (Joel 2:28-32) as being fulfilled in the events recorded in this chapter, and verses 25-28 where he says that David spoke about the resurrection (Psalm 16:8-11). Compare this to his understanding of Old Testament prophecy in 1 Peter 1:10-12. How does

this help our understanding of the Old Testament?

Prayer Pointers

❱ Thank God for the way that He is in the process of transforming your life.

❱ Pray that you might have boldness and opportunity to tell others about the Lord Jesus Christ.

❱ Ask God to help you have a deeper understanding about the way in which the Lord Jesus fulfils the Old Testament.

Day 6: Peter the preacher (2)

Read Acts 2

Return to verse 22 and reflect on what this tells us about the sovereignty of God, and responsibility of man. Meditate on verse 36.

Examine the response that Peter calls for in verse 38. Have you made this response yourself?

Prayer Pointers

❱ Use verse 36 as a vehicle for worship. Sing a song, or a hymn about the exaltation of the Lord Jesus.

❱ Pray that you may live a life of repentance, (turning away from sin and towards God), in the power of the Holy Spirit.

❱ Ask God to help you to make sure that you have placed everything in your life under the Lordship of Christ.

Day 7: Peter the Apostle

Peter's position in the early Church
Look at 1 Peter 1:1 to find out his position in the early church.

Read 1 Peter 5:1-5
These verses show us that as well as being one of the apostles he saw himself as an '*Elder*', who '*watched over*' the local Church. What does this tell you about his care for the Church, and how does it compare with your own?

Read Acts-1:12 –17
In these verses we see that Peter had a leading role in the very early days of the Church. Look at his description of the Word (16). How does your attitude to Scripture compare to Peter's? Think about the area of service that you are involved in and ask God to show you how much of it is grounded on His Word.

Prayer Pointers
▶ Thank God that He has made you part of His Church.
▶ Pray for your own Church's leaders. Pray that the qualities listed in 1 Peter 5.1-5 may be increasingly evident in their lives and ministries. Ask God to show you how you could encourage them.

Love: a theme study
The old song tells us that 'love is a many splendoured thing'; Christian love, however, is in a league of its own, and we are going to spend seven days exploring the character and the challenge of love.

Day 1: The God of love

It would be instinctive for us to go to the New Testament to explore this theme, but while love is one of the central messages of the New Testament it is not absent from the Old. God reveals Himself in both Testaments as a God of love. We are going to begin our exploration of this great theme by looking at a passage in the Old Testament in which God reveals Himself as a loving God.

Read Jeremiah 31:1-14, 6:1-5
The Prophet Jeremiah had the difficult task of warning the people of Judah that God's judgement was on its way. This judgement was to come in the form of an army from Babylon who were going to take them into exile. Look at the way that this is described in Jeremiah 6:1-5.
Compare it to the message about love and hope that is communicated in Jeremiah 31:1-14. How can you reconcile the two?

Identify the descriptions of the love of God in Jeremiah 31: 3, and think about the added meaning that the New Testament gives them.

Spend some time meditating on this description of Gods love.

Prayer Pointers

◗ Use Jeremiah 31: 3 as a basis for worship.

◗ Pray for your friends and family who do not know God's love, and pray that you may be made aware of opportunities to tell them about it.

◗ Pray for Christian friends who are going through difficult times and struggle to understand the love of God.

Day 2 : God's expression of love

Think back to yesterday's readings from Jeremiah. Were you able to reconcile the message of judgement with the message of love? If you were not able to, today's readings will help you.

Read Romans 5:8 and think about the way that God *demonstrates His own love to us.*

Turn to Isaiah 6:1-7, look at how the seraphim speak about the holiness of God, and think about the way that this makes Isaiah conscious of his own sinfulness.

Look at Romans 3:9-20 and consider the way in which sin separates us from God.

Meditate on Romans 5:8; reflect on the way in which it shows us that God has dealt with our sin, expressed His love to us and has remained consistent with His justice.

Prayer Pointers

◗ Begin by worshipping God for the love that he has shown to you in Christ.

◗ Confess your sins to Him, in the certain knowledge that they will be cleansed through the blood of Christ.

◗ Ask God to show you how to demonstrate His love to people you meet today.

Day 3: Christ's act of love

Today we are going to look atthe Cross from Christ's point of view, so that we can appreciate the cost and the depth of His love. We'll start by turning to some verses that tell us about the glory that He left behind. First, turn to Colossians 1:15-18. These verses tell us that Christ is the centre of the universe. When Paul tells us that He was *'first born over all creation'* he is not saying that Jesus is part of creation, he is describing His primacy over creation.

Now turn to Philippians 2:6-7 and think about the contrast between His heavenly splendour and His earthly humility.

In Mark 14:27-30 Jesus describes the suffering that He was to face; think of what this tells us of His sense of purpose.

Finally read Mark 15:16-41, pausing to thank the Lord Jesus for the expression of love that He has shown to you.

Prayer Pointers

▶ Praise God for the Cross and the effect that it has had on your life.

▶ Ask God to help you show the same kind of obedience that His Son showed.

▶ The verses in Colossians show us that Christ is the centre of the universe. Pray that Christ will be at the centre of your life, and ask your Heavenly Father to show you any area where this is not so.

Day 4: Loving God

Christianity is not a religion, it's a relationship founded on love. Having thought about the way that God has loved us; today we'll concentrate on our love for God.

Read Deuteronomy 6:4-9.

The idea of loving God is not confined to the pages of the New Testament; Deuteronomy 6:4-9 shows us that, in Old Testament times, it was an essential part of the relationship between God and His

people. Notice the distinction between heart, soul and might. The '**heart**' is the seat of the mind and the emotions, the '**soul**' is the source of life, vitality and being, while '**might**' speaks of strength, force and abundance. The combination of heart, soul and might speaks of an energetic and undivided love of God. Think about how this compares to your love of God; identify things that must change so that you can have this kind of love in your life.

Read Psalm 116.

This Psalm is an expression of the Psalmist's love for the Lord and he tells us about the way in which God initiated this relationship of love. Take a few moments to reflect on some of the things that God has done for you; then thank Him for them, and respond by expressing your love to Him.

Look at John 15:10 and identify the hallmark of our love for God. Does it show in your life?

Prayer Pointers

▶ Read the first two verses of Psalm 116 aloud, in an attitude of worship. Then pray them through in your own words.

▶ Pray about the areas in which you need to show your love for God, through obedience to His Word.

Day 5: Loving one another

It is easy to love someone who appeals to us, or who may be kind to us; it is a different matter when we come up against someone with whom we clash, or who may be cruel to us. Today we are going to spend time reading the words of John; the man who has been called 'the apostle of love.'
Read 1 John 3:10-18.
These verses give us some straight talking, but they need to be understood in the light of the situation in which John is writing.
He is writing to Christians who have suffered a terrible upset in their church. A number of people have broken away in pursuit of false teaching and have become arrogant about the spiritual heights, which they believed they had reached, and shown contempt towards those who have not followed them. John reassures the people to whom he writes, telling them that these loveless people were never Christians in the first place (see 2: 19).
It is clear that they have been struggling with the way that they have been treated by these people and have been tempted to respond in kind. Take a careful look at John's warning about hatred; is there anyone that you hate? Remember that John says this is inconsistent with someone who has *'passed from death to life'* (14).
John identifies love as the evidence of new birth; reflect on the connection between the two.
There is nothing sentimental about John's understanding of love. Look at the practical areas that he identifies, and think of ways in which they can be implemented in your life.

Prayer Pointers
▶ Praise God for your new birth; thank Him for the way in which this has given you a new nature that enables you to love others, as the Lord Jesus has loved you.
▶ Pray for that person (or those people), who make life difficult for you, asking God to enable you to show the same kind of sacrificial love that Christ displayed on the Cross.

Day 6: Forgiveness

The last time that Joseph saw his brothers they had thrown him into a pit and sold him into slavery. Years later, as Pharaoh's second in command, he comes face to face with them again. Genesis 45:1-15 recounts the touching scene of reconciliation, as Joseph shows that he has forgiven his brothers.
Read the passage through slowly, so that you can appreciate the drama and

the emotion of the occasion.

Reflect on the way that these events anticipate the Lord Jesus Christ.

Look for the ways in which Joseph makes his brothers feel at ease. What does this tell you about the way that you should treat someone who asks for your forgiveness?

Does Joseph say anything about the humiliation and distress that he suffered at their hands? Think about how this compares with the way you tell other people about things that have hurt you. What is the underlying truth that enables Joseph to show forgiveness? (Cf. Genesis 50:20-21, Psalm 105:16-20). How can this help you to handle the painful memories that you carry?

Day 7: A kaleidoscope of love

Read 1 Corinthians 13

1 Corinthians 13 is one of the most familiar passages in the Bible, but sometimes there is a danger that its true meaning can be lost in a sea of sentimentality. Read the chapter through, remembering that it is addressed to a Church riddled with division, and that it is set in the context of Paul's teaching about spiritual gifts. Verses 1-3 speak of the importance of love. Compare this to the priority that you place on love. What verdict does this have on your Christian work?

Read verses 4-7 slowly, identifying each element of love, and thinking of how you can display them.

What do verses 8-12 tell us about arguments that revolve around secondary issues?

Prayer Pointers

▶ Read verse 13 and thank God that His love never ends.

▶ Ask Him to help you to keep love as a priority in your life.

▶ Pray for someone you find difficult to love.

People in Prayer

I often tell my congregation that the best resource for prayer is to be found in the Bible. If you are struggling with prayer, you will draw great inspiration from the many prayers that can be found in God's Word. We are going to find this out for ourselves as we spend five days looking at Nehemiah's prayer.

Day 1: Surveying the circumstances

Today we are going to put Nehemiah's prayer into context, so we can understand its passion and power. Read 2 Chronicles 36:15-23, which provides us with a description of events leading up to the time in which Nehemiah prayed. The warnings sounded by the prophets had finally come true, the streets of Jerusalem were empty, the temple lay in ruins, and God's people had been taken captive and exiled to a foreign land. Decades later, Babylon, the land in which they were exiled, was conquered by Persia; and Cyrus, the King of Persia, allowed the Jews to return home.

What does this tell us about the way that God 'works all together for the good of those who love Him' (Romans 8:28)?

Prayer Pointers

▶ Praise God that He is always in control.
▶ Pray for a situation about which you feel helpless.
▶ Pray for anyone you know who is going through a difficult time.

Day 2: A man who cared

Today we'll move the clock forward more than 90 years. The Jews have returned to their homeland but Nehemiah has stayed in Shushan, the capital of the Persian Empire, where he is 'cupbearer to the king' (1:11). This involved him in sampling the wine that the king was to drink, primarily to test for poison. He receives some visitors from Jerusalem and is anxious for news of his people.

Read Nehemiah 4:1-4 taking special

note of his reaction to the bad news that he has been given. Look at the way that he channels this into prayer, how does it compare to the way that you receive bad news?

Read Psalm 112:7-8, what do these verses tell us about the condition of heart that is necessary for the kind of response that we read about in Nehemiah 1:4?

Prayer Pointers

▶ Read Romans 8:28 and praise God for the way in which 'all things work together for good to those who love God'

▶ Ask God to enable you to have a 'steadfast' and 'established' heart, so that you won't be 'afraid of evil tidings.'

Day 3: A man who worshipped

Today we are going to look at the way in which Nehemiah paused to worship God, before praying about the issues that troubled him.

Read the whole prayer out loud (Nehemiah 1:5-11), and then spend a few moments meditating on verse 5. Think about the way that, while the earthly situation looked grim, Nehemiah turned his eyes to heaven.

Read Deuteronomy 26:15 and think about the implications it has for the circumstances that Nehemiah faces.

Look at Matthew 6:9 for the way in which we are to pray along these lines. Take note of the way that Nehemiah shows a reverence of God, how does this compare to the reverence that you have for Him?

Prayer Pointers
▶ Use the verse 5 as a basis for a time to worship God.
▶ Pray the Lord's prayer out loud (Matthew 6:9-13), with a special emphasis on 'your kingdom come.'
▶ Ask God to help you to live in the light of His kingdom.

Day 4: A Man who Confessed

Read Nehemiah 1:7-9
Before Nehemiah prays about Jerusalem, he makes a confession of sin. What are the two major areas of failure that dominate his confession?
Read Deuteronomy 30:2-5, these verses contain the promise that Nehemiah uses as a basis for his prayer. What does this tell us about the importance of God's promises? What role should they play in our prayer lives?
Read 1 John 1:9, and confess your sin to the Lord, believing that 'He is faithful and just to forgive us our sins and to cleanse us from all unrighteousness.'

Prayer Pointers
▶ Praise God for the forgiveness that is available to us in Christ.
▶ Pray for your nation, with an awareness of sin and a longing for revival.

Day 5: Action Man

We are going to bring our meditation on Nehemiah's prayer to a close by looking at the way that he unleashes his prayer into action.
Read Nehemiah 1:10-11 and notice the way that Nehemiah reasserts the identity of God's people, and asks the LORD to be attentive to his prayer so that he might be given success.
Move on to Nehemiah 2:1-10 to see the way that Nehemiah stepped out in faith. Think about the way that you will need to translate your prayers into action.

Prayer Pointers
▶ Thank God that He is attentive to our prayers.
▶ Ask God to show you where you need to move from prayer to action.

The Big Picture
Our final approach to the quiet time will take the form of an overview of a book. We will be looking at the 'broad strokes' rather than the 'fine strokes' so that we can appreciate the way that Paul's letter to the Philippians has been put together.

Day 1: The Backstage View

Read Philippians 4:10-23
The closing verses of this book tell us about the series of events that brought Paul to write the letter.
Look at verse 14 to see what it tells us about Paul's personal circumstances. What does verse 18 tell us about the role of Epaphroditus? Think about the implications it has for the Christian approach to giving.
In verses 11-12 Paul expresses his gratitude for the gift, but he is quick to point out that he is not dependent upon it. Think about how we must be content in all circumstances, and look at verse 13 for the key to this contentment.

Prayer Pointers
▶ Give thanks that you can do 'all things through Christ who strengthens' you.
▶ Ask God to help you to use any circumstances you might face to learn to be content. Pray that you won't be infatuated by success or cast down by difficulties.

Day 2: Power through Prayer!

Read Philippians 1:3-8 and make a note of the way in which Paul expresses confidence in God, thanksgiving, and joy.
Look at the main concerns of Paul's

prayer in verses 9-11. Think about how this might help you to pray for your Church and for yourself.

Prayer Pointers
▶ Praise God that He has begun a work in you that He will complete at 'the day of Jesus Christ' (6).
▶ Give thanks for what He is doing in your local Church, and amongst your circle of Christian friends.
▶ Pray that God that might give you the qualities Paul speaks about in verses 9-11.

Day 3: Answers for concerned people

It looks as if Epaproditus brought two things from Philippi: a gift for Paul and a list of concerns! In the verses that we are looking at today Paul addresses their concern about his imprisonment and the possibility that he might be executed.

Read Philippians 1:12-14
When the Christians at Philippi heard that Paul was in prison, they would have wondered what was going on. Look at the way that Paul assures them that God has been working out His purposes, and reflect on how you can use the circumstances that God has put you in to tell others about the Lord Jesus.

Read Philippians 1:15-18

Some people didn't have a very positive attitude towards Paul and used his imprisonment to stir up trouble for him. Look at the way in which Paul accepts the situation, and draws something positive out of it.

Read Philippians 1:19-26

In view of the close bond between the Christians at Philippi and Paul, it is not surprising to learn that they were concerned about what was going to happen to him. Paul talks about his future in verses 19-26. Look at his central concern and compare it to your own.

Prayer Pointers

▶ Praise God that He can use your circumstances for His glory.

▶ Pray for people who are trying to make life difficult for you, ask God to overrule their plans, have His way and give you the attitude that is reflected in verse 18.

▶ Focus on your own attitude to life, compare it to the outlook reflected in verse 21, and ask God to bring your thinking into line with Paul's.

Day 4: Church Matters

Read Philippians 1:27-30

We are now in a new section of the letter.

In these verses, Paul tells the Philippians that he wants to hear about the progress that they are making.

Read Philippians 2:1-4

If they are to go forward in this way, they must work in harmony together.

Read Philippians 2:5-11

In order to achieve the harmony described in verses 1-4, they must follow the example of the Lord Jesus. Think about your determination to work with others in your church, and with other Christians in your workplace, school, college or neighbourhood. Is your main concern *'the faith of the Gospel?'*

Reflect on the relationships you have with other Christians. How might the attitude exemplified in the Lord Jesus transform your attitude towards them?

Prayer Pointers

▶ Praise the Lord Jesus for the way that He left His heavenly glory and took *'the form of the servant'* (2:7).

▶ Pray about the evangelistic work that your church is involved in.

▶ Spend some time praying about the relationships in your Church, and ask God to show you areas in which your attitude needs to change and become more Christ-like.

Day 5: Living the life

In the passage that we are looking at today, Paul turns to the practicalities of the principles that he has laid out in 2:1-11.

Read Philippians 2:12-18

Paul tells us to '*work out*' our salvation '*with fear and trembling*' (12), because God is already at work in us '*to will and to work on behalf of his good pleasure*' (13). List the practical things that this involves (14-17) and the lasting result of it (18).

Read Philippians 2:19-30

In these verses, Paul draws our attention to the example of two Christians: Timothy (19-24) and Epaphroditus (25-30). Look at the way that the example of these men illustrates the practical teaching given in verses 14-17, and the command in verses 12-13. Reflect on how you can follow their example.

Read Philippians 3:1

Paul brings this section to a close with a note of joy. Spend a few moments meditating on this, remembering that Paul is in prison as he writes it. What is the source of his joy?

Prayer Pointers

▶ Praise God that He is at work in you.

▶ Ask Him to help you to live as a '*blameless and harmless*' child of God '*without fault in the midst of a crooked and perverse generation*' (15). Be open to the Lord's conviction of any area in which your witness may be compromised.

Day 6: Negotiating danger zones

Today we are going to hear Paul sound a note of warning about spiritual dangers.

Read Philippians 3:2-11

The first source of danger stems from legalism and pride. Paul counters this with his own Christian experience.

Read Philippians 3:12-18

The second source of danger lies in the idea that one can reach a point of perfection in this life (12-18). Using his own experience as an example, Paul encourages us to '*press on towards the goal*'.

Read Philippians 3:19-21

The final danger is that Christians might depart from the Lord and return to the world. What does Paul use to counter this danger?

Read Philippians 4:1

In the light of these dangers, Paul concludes this part of the letter by calling us to '*stand fast in the Lord*'.

Revise each danger zone that Paul has marked out for us, and ask God to show you ways in which they relate to your life.

Meditate on verse 20, asking God to use this verse to give you an attitude about this life that is governed by an anticipation of heaven.

Prayer Pointers

▶ Praise God for the great future He has planned for you (21).

▶ Pray about areas of concern that have been highlighted by these three dangers.

Day 7: The Positive Path

In the last section of the letter, before expressing his thanks for the gift, Paul brings some final words of encouragement.

Read Philippians 4: 2 – 8

Firstly, Paul has to intervene in an argument that had become public knowledge (2-3). Then he calls us to 'rejoice in the Lord' (4), be gentle towards one another (5) and prayerful about the things that give us cause for concern or anxiety (6-7). The key to such a positive, spiritual outlook lies in the way that we think (8), and our obedience to God's Word (9).

If you are embroiled in a conflict with another Christian, think about the steps that you need to take in order to be able to 'agree in the Lord'. How does the positive thinking of verses 8-9 and the prayer of verses 6-7 help you?

Think about the pattern of prayer in verses 6-7; how will it help you to pray when you are worried?

Prayer Pointers

▶ Praise God for the joy and peace that He has given you in Christ.

▶ Bring your concerns to God, in the way that has been set out in verses 6-7.

▶ Pray for the person who you have found yourself in conflict with and ask God to help you both to 'agree in the Lord.'

Handle with Care!

The use and abuse of the Bible

When our children were at pre-school age, my wife was taken by surprise when the local Senior School telephoned. As the conversation went on, she realised that it had nothing to do with our children's education. The school wanted our help. One of the subjects taught at the School was 'child development', and as part of the course each pupil needed to spend several hours a week on a placement with a mother and a young child. My wife said that we were very happy to offer a placement in our home, and a week later a nervous looking teenager arrived at our door and introduced herself to us. In the weeks and months that followed, we got to know her quite well. One day she looked up at our mantelpiece and noticed a photograph of my graduation. 'What did your husband study?' she asked. When my wife told her that it was theology, she could see that this girl hadn't the first idea of what it was so she provided an explanation. She told her that theology is 'the study of God and the Bible'.

It is a pity that my University course didn't live up to that description! Nevertheless, it does tell us what theology should be; the very word has its origins in 'theos' which is Greek for 'God'. And the study of God can only be made through God's revelation given to us in the Bible. While a concordance and a notebook might be a great help to us, the Bible is essential to our quiet time. It is the place where God reveals Himself, unveils His plan, and shows us the way in which He works.

My children tell me that I often repeat myself, 'be careful with that, it's expensive,' I say. 'Yes dad, we know,' they reply, 'you've already told us!' I say this with such frequency because I know that if you do not appreciate the value of something you'll end up abusing it. In the same way, if we fail to appreciate the value of the Word of God, we won't handle it with the respect it deserves. In Old Testament times, the people of God were often reminded of the value of the Word. When they were about to take possession of the Promised Land, Moses told them to set up large stones on which they were to write 'all the words of this law.' (Deuteronomy 27:2-3,

8). At the very beginning of his rule, a King had to write down his own copy of the Law so that he could 'read it all the days of his life' (Deuteronomy 17:18-19). This principle wasn't limited to the King, the Word of God was to be so valued in the homes of ordinary people that it would be the major topic for discussion (Deuteronomy 6:7). And it was the neglect of the Word that led to deterioration in their relationship with God. This is what Hosea is talking about when he says the 'great things' that God had written 'were considered a strange thing' by His people (Hosea 8:12). Josiah became king of Judah at a time when the Word had fallen into such neglect that Hilkiah the priest emerged from the Temple saying 'I have found the book of the Law in the house of the LORD' (2 Chronicles 34:15). The New Testament tells us that these things 'were written down as warnings for us' (1 Corinthians 10:11, NIV), and they warn us about the danger of under-valuing the Word of God. We can act on this by drawing on the positive example set by David. He valued the Word so much that he said 'the law of your mouth is better to me than thousands of shekels of gold and silver' (Psalm 119:72). The Bible is priceless and, for that reason, we are going to spend this chapter thinking about the way in which we should handle it.

We are stewards of God's Word

In the closing days of his life a battle-hardened old preacher wrote a letter to a young pastor. The old preacher was the apostle Paul and the young Pastor was Timothy. Among the urgent instructions given, Paul tells Timothy to 'be diligent to present yourself approved to God, a worker who does not need to be ashamed, rightly dividing the word of truth' (2 Timothy 2:15). This presents an inspiring picture of a craftsman pouring his energy into a job that is going to be subject to inspection. The word 'approved' is translated from a Greek word which means to put something to the test and when you've found that it works you approve it, and 'rightly divide' speaks of accuracy and clarity. Literally, it means 'to cut straight.' Paul uses such a vivid image to make an important point; we must handle the Bible with immense care.

The Bible glorifies God

Book reviewers tell us that the first words of a novel often set the pace for the whole book. Whilst the Bible is no ordinary book the first few words, 'in the beginning God' (Genesis 1:1), sound the theme that runs from Genesis to Revelation. The Bible is a book about God! We seem to approach it from a different angle though; instead of looking at what it tells us about God, we channel all our thoughts into what it might be saying to us. Consequently, we have a poor understanding of the Bible's message. If this is something that you do, I don't want to discourage you, but I do want you to see that you are depriving yourself of the full riches yielded by the Word. It won't be too difficult to address the problem. When you read a passage through just keep one simple question in your mind: 'What does it tell me about God?' If you do this you'll be better equipped to understand what it says to you, because thinking about God will focus your mind on the main lessons that the passage has to teach.

The Bible's focus is Christ

When I first visited Israel, I was taken round a number of castles that had been built by the Crusaders. After we had seen the first two our guide asked us if we knew how to identify these buildings. One member of the group was quick to answer: 'Just look for the cross' he said. He was right; it is easy to spot a castle built by the Crusaders because their roofs are constructed in the shape of a cross. I can't pretend to have found these castles particularly inspiring but I have never forgotten their design, and it has often reminded me about the way that God has built His Word around the Lord Jesus.

Jesus is the focal point of the Bible because He is the centre of the universe. Paul tells that 'He is before all things and in Him all things consist' (Colossians 1:17), and John tells us that 'all things were made through Him and without Him nothing was made that was made' (John 1:3). When a Pharisee crept out under cover of darkness to speak with Jesus, he was told about the way in which God's plan revolves around His Son. Jesus told him that 'God so loved the world that He gave His only begotten Son, that whoever believes in Him should not perish but have everlasting life' (John 3:16). And when Paul writes to the Christians in Ephesus he declares Jesus to be the goal of history, saying: 'in the dispensation of the fullness of the times He (God) might gather together in one all things in Christ, both which are in heaven and which are on earth — in Him' (Ephesians 1:10).

If Jesus is the centre of the universe, the goal of history and the focal point of the Bible, He must be the key to understanding God's Word. In the early days of the Church an evangelist by the name of Philip had been led by the Holy Spirit to leave the blessings he enjoyed whilst preaching in Samaria, for the barrenness of a stretch of road that lay between Jerusalem and Gaza. When he was on this road, he met an Ethiopian official who was reading the following words from the book of Isaiah:

'He was led as a sheep to the slaughter;
And as a lamb before its shearer is silent,
So He opened not His mouth.
In His humiliation His justice was taken away.
And who will declare His generation?
For His life is taken from the earth' (Acts 8:32-33).

Philip asked him if he understood what he was reading. 'How can I unless someone guides me' he replied, so Philip came and sat down with him. 'I ask you' said the Ethiopian official 'of whom does the prophet say this, of himself or of some other man?' (Acts 8:34). Luke tells us that in response 'Philip opened his mouth, and beginning at this Scripture, preached Jesus to him' (Acts 8:35). The message is clear; we will only understand the Bible if we put Christ at the centre.

The Bible unfolds God's plan

One Sunday a family invited us to dinner. After we had eaten, cleared away, and washed up, I was shown a 'magic eye' poster. At first glance it looked like a mixture of different shapes and colours, but the theory is if you look more carefully you will see a picture hidden in the background. I was reliably told if I looked carefully enough I would see a picture of a Dolphin. 'I just can't see it,' I said, 'it looks like a lot of colourful shapes to me.' My guest was very persistent and he told me to stand back and look for the shape of the dolphin. Once I had identified the outline, the shapes fitted together, the colours fused, and I began to see the real picture. Sometimes the Bible can seem as confusing as a 'magic eye' poster, and when this happens we need a similar approach. We must stand back, look at the big picture, and put the passage we read into the context of the great plan that is unfolded from Genesis to Revelation.

A sketch of the scheme

Genesis recounts the creation of the world, the origins of the human race, the fall of man and the need for salvation. **Exodus and Numbers** show us how God gathered the descendants of Abraham together, freed them from slavery, led them out of Egypt and cared for them in the wilderness.

Leviticus provides the system of sacrifices and offerings by which people could approach God. **Deuteronomy** contains the final address delivered by Moses as the Israelites stood on the threshold of the Promised Land. In **Joshua,** we read about the way that God gives them conquest of Canaan, but in **Judges,** we are confronted by their failure. **Samuel, Kings and Chronicles** take us through the transition from the rule of Judges to the Monarchy, and finally to the exile. **Ezra and Nehemiah** introduce us to a chastened people who return to God, go back to their homes and rebuild their nation. The **Psalms** and **Wisdom** literature give an added depth to the way that God's plan is unfolded. Finally, **the prophets** reveal God's Word, warn of His judgement, and look forward to national restoration and the coming of Christ.

In the New Testament, the **Gospels** declare the good news of Christ's life, death, and resurrection. **Acts** shows us the way in which the Holy Spirit continues Christ's work in the Early Church. **The letters** address practical and doctrinal issues, and **Revelation** sets our sights on the triumphant outcome of the final conflict and the certainty of Christ's return.

This is only a brief sketch, but it does present the major movements of God's plan. He created the world, gathered His people, cared for them, and dealt with them by taking them from their homeland to purge them of their idols. After this, He brought them home and the scene was set for the New Testament. Jesus was born; He chose His disciples, preached the good news, and fulfilled the promises that had been made by the prophets. His death and resurrection made the sacrificial system redundant and He ascended into heaven sending the Holy Spirit to continue His work and promising to return.

THE UNIQUENESS OF THE BIBLE

Many authors but one source

A very keen Christian once asked me an intriguing question. 'I want to know what God thinks. Can you tell me how I can find out?' I don't think he was expecting the answer that I gave Him; I told him to read his Bible. 'The Bible is full of God's thoughts,' I said, 'go and see for yourself.'

In Paul's second letter to Timothy we are told that 'all Scripture is given by inspiration of God' (2 Timothy 3:16). The word translated 'inspired' is made up of two Greek words, one meaning 'God' and the other 'to breathe'. Literally, Paul is saying that all Scripture is 'God-breathed'. If this is so, why do we find so many different styles in the Bible? This is something that Peter addresses when he tells us that 'prophecy never came by the will of man, but holy men of God spoke as they were moved by the Holy Spirit' (2 Peter 1: 21). The word 'moved' speaks of something or someone being carried along. You'll find the same word used in Acts to describe the way that a ship was carried along by the wind (Acts 27:15,17). Explaining the significance of this word Michael Green says: 'the Prophets raised their sails, so to speak (they were obedient and receptive), and the Holy Spirit filled them and carried their craft along in the direction He wished: men spoke: God spoke.'[24] The personality, and the style of each writer was under the control and guidance of the Holy Spirit yielding the rich tapestry of history, poetry, law, prophecy and teaching that we find in the Bible.

Different cultures but a timeless message

When I was a young Christian I was warned against being 'unequally yoked with unbelievers.' This confused me; as far as I was concerned, a yolk was something in the middle of an egg. What did it mean? My problem lay in the fact that this instruction[25] was originally given to people who were familiar with the sight of two oxen yoked together in order to pull a plough. If the two animals were not equal in height and size, the yoke wouldn't fit, the plough wouldn't work, and the job wouldn't get done. This picture relates to the culture to which it was originally addressed, but the message is timeless; we mustn't allow ourselves to get involved in relationships that tie us to the world, especially marriage to someone who is not a Christian.

The context of the Bible is not limited to one particular culture. Abraham lived in a different culture from Moses, and Ezekiel declared God's Word in a different culture from Jeremiah. We must not think that this makes the Bible impossible to understand! On the contrary, it should make us confident about the timelessness of the Word of God.

Different situations but one scheme

A school teacher I knew was once asked whether she could recommend a book that could provide some exciting stories which would capture children's imagination. 'No problem' she said 'the Bible is full of them.' Just think about the number of dramatic, real-life stories contained in the Bible. A young man is kidnapped by his brothers, sold into slavery, thrown into prison and then catapulted to power (Joseph). An angel visits the most insignificant person of the most insignificant tribe and tells him that he has been chosen to defeat the vicious enemy who has oppressed his people for decades (Gideon). A religious leader who tries to stamp out the church, imprison their leaders and scatter them across the country has his life turned upside down when Christ intercepts his journey to Damascus (Saul of Tarsus). These are just a handful of examples; I could fill page after page with them. The Bible recounts many different situations but it reveals one divine plan that is fulfilled in Christ.

Shortly after I became a Christian I attended a meeting that had been arranged by an organisation working with Christians in the former Communist bloc. A Christian, simply known as 'Brother Alexander', told us about the pressures that he, and other believers in his land, faced. I found myself particularly moved by his description of the way in which they received a delivery of Bibles that had been smuggled into their country. It sounded like a delivery of food to people who had been suffering from famine. They had been deprived of God's Word for so long that, as soon as a Bible fell into their hands, they devoured as much of it as they could. I came away from the meeting realising the value of God's Word and thankful for the freedom I had to read it whenever I wanted to. We don't know how long we will have such freedom, but while we do let's be sure to treasure God's Word and handle it with care!

A Tour of the Terrain

Appreciating the diversity of the Bible

When we first moved to Portsmouth, a family was kind enough to spend a day showing us around the city. We were taken to a public garden for a picnic lunch, to the sea walls to experience the coast, and to the harbour to look at the ships. It was a relaxed but brief tour of the city and, while it was a great help to us, it took more than a day before we felt confident that we could find our own way around. This chapter is similar to that day's orientation; we are going to spend some time surveying the Bible, but it will only be a brief tour designed to give us a taste of the variety of literature we find in the Word of God.

Taking the Labour out of the Law

Many people emerge from reading the books that contain the law with a sigh of relief. This is hardly surprising when you consider the intricacies of the ceremonies, sacrifices, laws and offerings they have read about, but the law is part of the Word of God and it shouldn't be ignored. The law might seem to be difficult and involved, but it's not impossible to understand. Let's spend a little time thinking about its place in the Bible so that we can take the labour out of the law.

When we read the chapters that contain the law the question often lurking at the back of our minds is, 'what does this have to do with me?' And the answer we arrive at will affect the way we understand the law and the Bible. If we decide it is restricted to a civilisation far removed from ours and has nothing to do with us, we will find these books very difficult. The good news, however, is that the law is relevant to us, although it doesn't have the same application as it had in the days before Christ's death and resurrection; we are able to see it in a different light.

In a village where I once lived, I used to walk past a derelict house. Eventually, it became the property of a builder who demolished it and built a new house on the site. At first, I would walk by to see the workmen laying the new foundations; later I noticed they had assembled the structure. By then, it was possible to discern the shape and the size of the house, but it was far from complete. Eventually the house was finished. It was the same building, which I had seen on every other occasion, but now it was complete. When we read the details of the laws, sacrifices, and ceremonies in the Old Testament, we are not reading of something unrelated to the New Testament. Like that house; the law lays the foundations and constructs a framework but, in Christ, the work is complete.

The people who were given these laws might seem a world removed from us, but if we read the law carefully we will see that, like us, they had a relationship with God which was founded on His grace. The Ten Commandments are introduced with the words: 'I am the LORD your God, who brought you out of the land of Egypt, out of the house of bondage' (Exodus 20:2). This was designed to remind them that they had already been redeemed, and to motivate them to obey the commands. The system of sacrifices and ceremonies might look a little daunting to us, but we mustn't forget that they find their fulfilment in the death of Christ.

The law is set in the context of a relationship, which God had established with His people, a relationship so special it is called a **covenant**. In the Bible, a covenant describes a 'divinely imposed legal agreement between God and man that stipulates the conditions of their relationship.'[26] The description shows us the way in which two parties are involved, but it rules out the idea that man can negotiate the terms of the covenant, because it is 'divinely imposed.'[27] At the end of Leviticus the people of Israel are presented with a clear choice, they can experience the blessings that come from obedience, or punishment that will follow disobedience. In both cases, God speaks about the covenant He has established.

'You shall not make idols for yourselves; neither a carved image nor a sacred pillar shall you rear up for yourselves; nor shall you set up an engraved stone in your land, to bow down to it; for I am the LORD your God. You shall keep My Sabbaths and reverence My sanctuary: I am the LORD.
If you walk in My statutes and keep My commandments, and perform them, then I will give you rain in its season, the land shall yield its produce, and the trees of the field shall yield their fruit. Your threshing shall last till the time of vintage, and the vintage shall last till the time of sowing; you shall eat your bread to the full, and dwell in your land

safely. I will give peace in the land, and you shall lie down, and none will make you afraid; I will rid the land of evil beasts, and the sword will not go through your land. You will chase your enemies, and they shall fall by the sword before you. Five of you shall chase a hundred, and a hundred of you shall put ten thousand to flight; your enemies shall fall by the sword before you.
For I will look on you favourably and make you fruitful, multiply you and confirm My covenant with you. (Leviticus 26:1-9)

'I also will do this to you: I will even appoint terror over you, wasting disease and fever which shall consume the eyes and cause sorrow of heart. And you shall sow your seed in vain, for your enemies shall eat it. I will set My face against you, and you shall be defeated by your enemies. Those who hate you shall reign over you, and you shall flee when no one pursues you…. But for their sake I will remember the covenant of their ancestors, whom I brought out of the land of Egypt in the sight of the nations, that I might be their God: I am the LORD.' (Leviticus 26:16-17, 45)

Having thought about the relevance of the law, we can begin to appreciate the way in which it addresses different aspects of life in Old Testament times.

It provides a system of **sacrifices and ceremonies** that reach their fulfilment in the death of Christ. Brian Edwards tells us that 'every detail of the Old Testament law was pointing like a signpost towards Christ … He is our altar and our offering for sin. When we place our trust in Christ for salvation we are fulfilling all of this part of the law, because it was wholly completed in Christ.'[28]

The law also addressed **national life,** regulating commerce, implementing justice, identifying criminal behaviour, and prescribing punishment. At Mount Sinai God told the Israelites that they were to become 'a kingdom of priests and a holy nation' (Exodus 19:6). One of the roles of a priest was to represent God to the people, and the law governing national life provided the means for the Israelites to become 'a kingdom of priests' (Exodus 19:6) and 'a light to the Gentiles' (Isaiah 49:6). When they obeyed the law, they were fulfilling God's will and glorifying Him among the nations around them. Naturally, when we read such laws we cannot apply them in the same way as they were used in Old Testament times but, like the Israelites, we belong to 'a kingdom of priests'. Peter says 'you are a chosen generation, a royal priesthood, a holy nation, His own special people, that you may proclaim the praises of Him who called you out of darkness into His marvellous light' (1 Peter 2:9). When we read the laws that regulated national life, we should keep their greater purpose in mind and consider what they have to say about the way in which we represent the Lord in our community.

Food and hygiene are very topical issues in our society, but when we read the Old Testament, we can see that they are not issues confined to the late twentieth and early twenty-first centuries. There are laws relating to the carcasses of dead animals (Leviticus 11:24-30), infectious skin diseases (Numbers 5:2), sanitation (Deuteronomy 23:12-13), and the designation of which foods are 'clean' and which are 'unclean' (Leviticus 11:2, Deuteronomy 14:21). You might read such laws and ask what they have to do with us when Christ has 'declared all foods clean' (Mark 7:19 NIV). It is true to say they no longer impose a binding obligation upon us, but they do present a timeless principle. In the same way that God's people were to keep every area of their lives undefiled, we are called to 'cleanse ourselves from all filthiness of the flesh and spirit, perfecting holiness in the fear of God' (2 Corinthians 7:1).

The Ten Commandments represents the **moral law**. In this part of the law God lays down a 'permanent and perpetual relationship that must always exist between Himself and man.'[29] These commands have a direct bearing upon us and, like David, we should meditate on them day and night (Psalm 119:97). On this side of the death and resurrection of the Lord Jesus Christ, we are in a better position to put them into practice, because God has put His Holy Spirit within us and fulfilled His promise to write the law on our hearts (Jeremiah 31:33).

So, how can we take the labour out of the law? Here are some principles that will help us to navigate our way through this difficult part of God's Word.

First, we should think about the way in which the particular law we are reading functioned in the life of the people of God. Did it regulate their national life? Was it concerned with health and hygiene? Does it lay down the way that people were to worship God? Is it one of the Ten

Commandments, or does it amplify one of them? This will help us to understand its significance and to see the way that it relates to us.

Secondly, we should reflect on what it tells us about Israel's relationship with God. The law is not a collection of rules laid down for the Israelites; it established the boundary lines of their relationship with God.

Thirdly, we should meditate on the things that it tells us about God. We can think about the way in which laws demanding justice reflect His righteousness, that laws about hygiene mirror His holiness, and the way in which laws about sacrifices and offerings show us how He hates sin, but provides a way for us to receive forgiveness.

Fourthly, we should consider whether the law we are reading about acts as a signpost to the Lord Jesus.

Finally, we should identify the timeless principles that should be put into practice.

Persisting with the Prophets

If you find the Law the most difficult part of the Bible, the prophets will probably follow a close second. Sometimes the sheer size of a book like Jeremiah or Ezekiel can be enough to dent the enthusiasm of the most determined Bible reader, and we may often find ourselves struggling to understand its meaning. The prophets are not for the fainthearted, but they will be a great help to us if we persist with them. Let's think about how we can do so.

Understand the nature of prophecy

Some people understand prophecy as a form of prediction, but this is a very unsatisfactory description of prophecy in the Old Testament. A Prophet would often introduce his message by saying 'thus says the Lord' (Isaiah 44:2) because he was proclaiming the Word of God. This is not to say there was no element of prediction in his message. Habakkuk foretold the exile to Babylon (Habakkuk 1), and Isaiah and Jeremiah spoke about the approach of exile and looked forward to the return home (Isaiah 49, Jeremiah 30). A great proportion of a prophet's message, however, addressed the failure of God's people to observe their part of the covenant. They were the 'watchdogs of the society of God's people ... They call people back to faithful obedience to the covenant.'[30] Indeed, it was the failure of God's people to heed these warnings that led to their defeat at the hands of their enemies. Beyond this, the Prophets looked forward to the end of judgement and to national and spiritual restoration. For example, after painting a vivid picture of the inescapable judgement that was to come upon Israel, Amos speaks of a day of unparalleled blessing. This would be a day when 'the plowman shall overtake the reaper, And the treader of grapes him who sows seed; The mountains shall drip with sweet wine, And all the hills shall flow with it ' (Amos 9:13). Jeremiah talks about 'the whirlwind of the Lord' and 'the fierce anger of the Lord' which 'will not return until He has done it, and until He has performed the intents of His heart' (Jeremiah 30:23-24). In the verses that follow, however, there is a dramatic change of tone when God declares He has loved His people 'with an everlasting love' and promises that the nation will be rebuilt (Jeremiah 31: 3-4). These promises were partially fulfilled when the Jews left Babylon and returned to their homeland, but their complete fulfilment is found in the New Covenant that God has established through the Lord Jesus Christ. We see this in Acts, when the leaders of the Early Church met at Jerusalem and Peter said that a prophecy given by Amos (Amos 9:11-12) was fulfilled by Gentiles coming into the Church.

'And with this the words of the prophets agree, just as it is written: "After this I will return And will rebuild the tabernacle of David, which has fallen down. I will rebuild its ruins, And I will set it up, so that the rest of mankind may seek the LORD, Even all the Gentiles who are called by My name, Says the LORD who does all these things." "Known to God from eternity are all His works." Therefore I judge that we should not trouble those from among the Gentiles who are turning to God" (Acts 15:15-19).

Understand the role of a prophet
We associate sixteen books with the prophets. Four of them, Isaiah, Jeremiah, Ezekiel, and Daniel are 'Major Prophets'. And twelve, Hosea, Joel, Amos, Obadiah, Jonah, Micah, Nahum, Habakkuk, Zephaniah, Haggai, Zechariah, and Malachi, are 'Minor Prophets'. This distinction is based on the lengths of the books rather than the significance of their message.

The basic Old Testament word for prophet means a 'spokesman' or a 'speaker'. Essentially, it describes a person who is authorised to speak on behalf of another, and the Old Testament prophets were authorised to speak on behalf of God. Prophets are also described as 'seers' (1 Samuel 9:19), 'messengers' (Haggai 1:13) and 'men of God' (1 Samuel 2:27), but every description emphasises the fact that God had called them to proclaim His Word.

Measure the medium

When we read the words of a prophet it is important to remember that their first listeners didn't read their words—they heard them, and sometimes they even saw the message put into action! For example, Amos presents his message in the form of a series of riddles (Amos 3:3-6), and then in the form of a funeral dirge (Amos 5:1-15). And Ezekiel acts out the forthcoming siege of Jerusalem by lying on his right side for forty days (Ezekiel 4:6).

In addition to familiar forms and visual aids, the prophets also used vivid images. Joel describes a plague of 'chewing', 'swarming', and 'crawling' locusts (Joel 1: 1-4). Zechariah recounts a vision of a flying scroll that symbolised a curse that God was sending 'out over the face of the whole earth' (Zechariah 5:1-4). Jeremiah talks about mountains that tremble and hills that sway (Jeremiah 4:24). These images would have been powerful tools that would have captured the listeners' attention and communicated the prophets' message.

Think three dimensionally

One of the reasons why we struggle to understand the prophets may be because we have a one-dimensional view; we are only interested in what they say to us. This needs to be replaced with three-dimensional thinking. First, we should look at the world in which the prophet lived. Although their messages had far reaching implications, they were rooted in events of their own time, and they had important things to say to their own people. Secondly, we should consider whether it says anything about the life and ministry of the Lord Jesus Christ. It may contain a direct reference, it may be an indirect signpost, or it may not imply anything; but it must be taken into account. Thirdly, we should determine whether it says anything about the return of Christ. Although there are many prophecies that have been fulfilled by the birth, death, and resurrection of Christ, some are not yet completely fulfilled. Having worked through these three dimensions, we will find ourselves in a better position to understand the prophet's message, see how it relates to us, and respond to its challenge.

Praising with the Psalmist

One of the great attractions of the Psalms is the way they communicate the Word of God through human experience. The Reformer John Calvin described them as 'an anatomy of all parts of the soul; for which there is not an emotion of which any can be conscious that is not here represented as in a mirror.'[31] From the cry 'have mercy on me O God, according to your loving kindness' (Psalm 51:1), and the anguished question 'will the Lord cast off for ever?' (Psalm 77:7) to the triumphant exclamation 'make a joyful shout to the Lord all you lands' (Psalm 100:1), the Psalms are at hand to enable us to work things through, wrestle with doubt and fear, and give voice to our praise.

The Puritan Matthew Henry introduced his commentary on the Psalms by saying 'there is no one book of scripture that is more helpful to the devotions of the saints than this.'[32] The Psalms provide us with a storehouse of different kinds of prayers, poems, and songs. Some sound a call to worship, and celebrate the goodness of God. Others are written in desperate circumstances expressing fear or sorrow, and others provide practical teaching. If we draw on their vast resources, we shall find that our quiet times will be greatly enriched.

Walking in wisdom

In our minds, wisdom is associated with learning, experience, or age, but in the Old Testament, it is perceived as something that originates with God. Solomon described wisdom as something that God had built into the order of the universe: 'The LORD by wisdom founded the earth' (Proverbs 3:19). Wisdom literature is provided to enable us to find our place within this ordered system, and when we find it, we will be able to make the right choices and lead lives which are pleasing to the Creator.

Four books fall into this classification. **Ecclesiastes** is a cyclical discourse written by a man known as 'the teacher' who grapples with the issues of life 'under the sun' (Ecclesiastes 1:3). **Proverbs** concentrates on practical issues establishing clear guidelines for a lifestyle that is pleasing to God. It also presents a sharp contrast between wisdom and folly. **Job** reflects on circumstances in which this world order becomes distorted and the righteous person finds himself disorientated, because of the suffering that has been unleashed into his life. And the **Song of Songs** is a love poem composed by Solomon revolving around the relationship between a bridegroom and his bride.

The wisdom books bring an added dimension to God's Word. They invite us to explore issues such as suffering, injustice, sexuality, morality, honesty, and integrity. They are relevant to the ethical dilemmas that we face and they will stimulate us to approach them from a biblical perspective. Derek Kidner compares these books to other parts of the Old Testament saying: 'The blunt "thou shalt" or "shalt not" of the Law, and the urgent 'Thus saith the Lord' of the Prophets, are joined now by the cooler comments of the teacher and the often anguished question of the learner.'[33]

Whilst the Old Testament tells us that 'the Lord by wisdom founded the earth' (Proverbs 3:19) the New Testament shows us that it reaches its crescendo in Christ. In Him 'are hidden all treasure of wisdom' (Colossians 2:3) and He 'became for us wisdom from God' (1 Corinthians 1:30). Where do we locate this wisdom? At the Cross!

'We preach Christ crucified, to the Jews a stumbling block and to the Greeks fool-ishness, but to those who are called, both Jews and Greeks, Christ the power of God and the wisdom of God. Because the foolishness of God is wiser than men, and the weakness of God is stronger than men' (1 Corinthians 1:23-25).

Now that we have thought about the character and the content of the wisdom books, we'll establish some guidelines to help us to get the most from them.

First, it is important that we understand the passage we read in the light of the overall scheme of the book. This is particularly important with Job, which contains an introductory narrative (Job 1-2), three cycles of speeches (Job 4-14, 15-21, 22-26), three monologues (Job 29-31, 32-37, 38-42.6) and a conclusion (Job 42:7-17) .34 Similarly, Ecclesiastes is composed of an introduction (Ecclesiastes 1:1-11), two discourses (Ecclesiastes 1:12-11:6, 11:7-12:7), a reiteration of the theme (Ecclesiastes 12:8), and a conclusion (Ecclesiastes 12:9-14). A good Study Bible or commentary that provides an outline of each book will help us to do this.

Secondly, we must keep track of the way that the passage or book develops. It is dangerous to isolate verses or chapters when they are part of a highly structured argument. Most of us will not read a book in a single sitting, so it will be important to make sure that we don't lose the logical development. This is a matter of keeping a note of where the book has taken us and reviewing it before we read a fresh passage.

Thirdly, we should think about the broader context. The Old Testament concept of wisdom presents an ordered system that God has woven into the fabric of the universe. The New Testament shows us that this wisdom is embodied in the Lord Jesus Christ and encountered at the Cross. This is the wider concept within which we should understand and apply the Word of God in Job, Proverbs, Ecclesiastes, and the Song of Songs.

Navigating Old Testament Narrative

It had been a lively evening service; the Congregation had closed their hymn books, opened their Bibles and were looking expectantly to the preacher. 'My text tonight is first Kings nineteen verse four,' he said, 'he came and sat down under a juniper tree.' As this particular preacher had been known to extract interesting sermons from the most obscure parts of the Bible, the people listened with interest. 'I looked up the meaning of Juniper tree in my Strong's concordance,' he said with an air of wisdom, 'it is a kind of broom plant.' The Congregation began to look a little confused but they patiently waited for the practical point. 'Friends' he said, his voice rising to a crescendo 'let God sweep your troubles away.'

I wonder how we would react if we were to be on the receiving end of this kind of approach to Scripture. I think most of us would probably fight off the temptation to snigger, shake our heads in disbelief, and declare it a clumsy misuse of the Bible. However, we might find that we are adopting the same kind of approach as this hapless preacher when we read Old Testament narrative. And we do so when we read a passage for the sole purpose of extracting a few practical lessons for ourselves.

The historical books[35] present an accurate record of the history of God's people, but their main purpose is to help us understand the way God dealt with His people and worked out His purposes. Consequently, before we look for practical lessons, we should think about what each passage tells us about these. In order to do this we will need a basic understanding of the major events in the Old Testament, and these are listed below:

▶ The Creation and Fall (Genesis 1-3)
▶ The Flood (Genesis 6-9)
▶ The Tower of Babel (Genesis 11)
▶ The Promises given to the Patriarchs (Genesis 12-50)
▶ The Exodus from Egypt (Exodus 1-15)
▶ The Wilderness Wanderings (Exodus 15-20, Numbers)
▶ The Conquest of the Promised Land (Joshua)
▶ The Days of the Judges (Judges and Ruth)
▶ The United Kingdom (1 Samuel 10 – 1 Kings 11)
▶ The Divided Kingdom (1Kings 12–2 Kings 24, 2 Chronicles 10-36:14)
▶ The Exile (2 Kings 25, 2 Chronicles 36:15-23)
▶ The Return (Ezra, Nehemiah, Esther)

As well as showing us how God deals with His people, Old Testament narrative anticipates Christ, so we should always think about the passage that we are reading in the light of the person and work of Jesus. Sometimes it will glow with an anticipation of the Lord Jesus, but other times the link may not be so easy to identify. I found a comment made by Bible teacher David Jackman very helpful. He talked about incidents that we read about in a book like Judges, where 'everyone did what was right in his own eyes' (Judges 17:6), reminding us these incidents anticipate Christ in the way they expose the flaws of human leadership and look forward to His perfect rule.

Having thought along these lines, we will be in a far better position to understand the real practical teaching contained in the passage that we read.

Gleaning from the Gospels

After reading books like Leviticus, Ezekiel or Job we could be forgiven for turning to the Gospels with a sigh of relief. After all, it was the Gospels that introduced us to the Christian life and to the Lord Jesus Himself. There is no doubt that we have come to one of the easier parts of the Bible, but as the old saying goes 'familiarity breeds contempt', and it is in familiar territory that we might be most prone to make mistakes.

Although they include biographical details, the Gospels are not biographies of Jesus. The Greek word that translates 'good news' or 'gospel' was a new word chosen to describe a unique type of literature. Matthew, Mark, Luke and John called their books 'gospels' because they were associated with **the** gospel that was being enthusiastically and courageously preached by the early Christians. And the Gospel writers rooted this message in historical accounts of the life and ministry of Jesus. Matthew, Mark, Luke, and John are not dispassionate biographers—they are evangelists. John said his Gospel was 'written that you may believe that Jesus is the Christ, the Son of God, and that believing you may have life in His name' (John 20:31).

When we steer our quiet times into the familiar territory of the Gospels, we need to handle them with the same kind of care that we have shown in other areas of the Bible. To exercise this care there are several things we should bear in mind.

Each Gospel has a framework

Matthew, Mark, Luke, and John wrote their Gospels, under the guidance and inspiration of the Holy Spirit, with a clear structure in mind. **Matthew** introduces us to his gospel with the nativity of Jesus and then alternates between sections of Jesus' teaching and narrative, concluding with Jesus' death and resurrection and the great commission. **Mark** divides his Gospel into two parts; in the first (1:1 – 8:30) he focuses on the identity of Jesus, which is finally revealed in Peter's words 'you are the Christ' (Mark 8:29). This ushers us into the second half of the Gospel (8:31-16:8) where the emphasis is placed upon the work that Jesus came to do. **Luke's Gospel** moves in five phases covering the infancy of Jesus (1:1-4.13), His ministry in Galilee (4:14-9-50), His journey to Jerusalem (9:51-19:44) His ministry in

Jerusalem (19:45-22:53) and His death and resurrection (23:1-24:53). **John** also divides his Gospel into two parts, and they can be summarised by the statement made by Jesus in John 16:28: 'I came forth from the Father and have come into the world. Again, I leave the world and go to the Father.' The first half of the Gospel (chapters 1-11) shows that Jesus is the Christ and the Son of God who has come from His father in heaven to reveal Himself to us. And the second (12-21) portrays Jesus as the Son returning to His Father.[36]

Each Gospel has an emphasis

An Aunt of mine lived in a house on the corner of a busy road and it became the scene of many accidents. I remember several occasions where her garden wall had been damaged because vehicles had crashed into it. The Police promptly arrived on the scene to take statements from witnesses. The person standing nearest to the house could describe the accident from where he stood, the person standing over the road could add some extra detail, and my aunt herself could describe the sights and the sounds from her unique vantage point. A combination of the three accounts would provide the Police with all the details that they needed for their investigations. God has given us four Gospels that combine to tell us everything that we need to know about the life, death, resurrection, and ascension of the Lord Jesus. Each Gospel has a distinctive emphasis; Mark portrays Jesus as a servant, John concentrates on Jesus as the Son of God, Matthew focuses on Jesus as the King, and Luke on Jesus as the perfect man.

As we work through a Gospel, we will read about miracles, teaching, parables, and narrative. The narrative sets the pace of each Gospel, the miracles declare Jesus' power and divinity, the teaching lays the foundations of the New Covenant and the parables spring the unexpected upon us.

Living in the letters

When you turn to the letters, you may feel as if you are opening someone else's mail! The earliest verses you will read address themselves to specific people; 'to the saints who are in Ephesus' (Ephesians 1:1) or 'to all the saints in Christ Jesus who are in Philippi' (Philippians 1:1).

It is true that the letters have been written to certain people in particular situations, but they are not private correspondence. Paul, who wrote many such letters, usually starts by introducing himself as an apostle. He begins his letter to Timothy with the words: 'Paul, an apostle of Jesus Christ, by the commandment of God our Saviour and the Lord Jesus Christ.' (1 Timothy 1:1). And Colossians opens with the statement: 'Paul, an apostle of Jesus Christ by the will of God.' (Colossians 1:1). Paul begins his letters in this way to remind us that he is an apostle who has been entrusted with God's Word.

Although the letters are targeted at specific issues and problems faced by the early churches, the message of each letter has a much wider audience. They are the property of the whole Church and their message is relevant to us.

In order to hear the message of each letter clearly we will need to be aware of the circumstances to which it was originally addressed. When we read 1 John, we will be better equipped to understand what he is saying when we put ourselves in the position of the Christians to whom he writes. They were shocked by the departure of people who had left their Churches in pursuit of false teaching (see 1 John 2:19) and they found themselves lacking in their assurance. Galatians can be better understood by identifying a group of people who had arrived in Galatia and told the church they must be circumcised. Paul regarded this as another gospel (Galatians 1:8) and engages in a passionate argument in the defence of the doctrine of justification by faith alone.

Sometimes we can treat the letters of the New Testament as a collection of thoughts, challenges, and exhortations and ignore the way that they unfold a logical argument, but we do so to our loss. Granted, some letters might be easier to follow than others, but it is important to keep track of the direction of the argument and the development of the theme of each book.

Accessing Acts

Of all the books in the Bible, Acts must be in the running to be the most dynamic. In the course of its twenty eight chapters Luke describes a mission that began in Jerusalem, moved out to Samaria and embraced 'the ends of the earth' (Acts 1:8). The journey from Jerusalem 'to the end of the earth' takes us through some varied scenery: we read powerful sermons and speeches from the lips of Peter, Stephen, and Paul. We are given personal accounts of the journeys that Luke took with Paul, and we are the unseen listener at some crucial consultations determining the direction of the Church (Acts 15:1-29).

The Acts of the Apostles is the second part of a two-volume work composed by Luke. The first volume is his Gospel, where we see Jesus carry out His ministry with the disciples alongside Him. The second volume is Acts where we see Jesus ascend to heaven and continue His work in the Early Church by the power of the Holy Spirit.

Two men dominate the Acts of the Apostles. The first is **Peter**, who is the leading figure in the first twelve chapters of the book. In these chapters, Luke shows us the way in which the Church grew from its early Jewish roots. The second is **Paul** under whose ministry the Church expands to a world-wide movement that is largely made up of Gentiles.

There are three tools that will help us to tap the riches of Acts. First, we should think about the way in which Luke traces the advance of the Gospel. Some people do this by dividing the book into three parts relating to the way that the Gospel is preached in Jerusalem (1-7), spreads to Samaria (8-10), and reaches 'the ends of the earth' (11-28). Secondly, we should unearth Luke's teaching. As well as being a historian, Luke is an evangelist and a teacher, and he has written his book to inform and instruct. Thirdly, we must be sure to link the things that we read about with other parts of the New Testament. It is dangerous to take a description of something that happens in Acts as a principle that should be put into practice today. Some things that Luke describes carry over, but they are confirmed by the instruction of other parts of the New Testament. For example, Timothy, and Titus speak of the appointment of Deacons and Elders, but the use of lots to choose a successor to Judas (Acts 1:15-26) is something that is not confirmed in any other part of the New Testament and should not be put into practice today.

Strictly speaking, Acts is a historical book about the origins of the Church, but it should not be treated like a Church handbook. The distin-guished Presbyterian Professor, J. Gresham Machen, said 'the author of Acts is concerned with the extensive rather than with the intensive progress of the Church – with the winning of new converts rather than with questions of principle or morals or policy.' [37] In Acts, Luke provides a breathtaking overview of the way in which the Gospel of Christ, presented in his first volume, has spread throughout the known world.

Wrestling with Revelation

My friends and I had finally seen an answer to our prayers; the Christian Union was holding its first meeting. The classroom was comfortably full and the teacher who helped us to get it off the ground was helping us put a programme together. 'What sort of things would you like to discuss?' he asked. A hand shot up in the air 'Can we look at the third antichrist, sir?' said an earnest looking young man. 'The third what?' asked the teacher. 'The third antichrist sir! The first one was Hitler, the second was Stalin and the third hasn't arrived on the scene yet.' By now my friends and I were showing signs of impatience and even frustration, but our teacher kept a cool head. 'You know, Smith,' he said to the boy concerned, 'it's amazing the things that we can read into the book of Revelation.'

I have to say that out of all the Biblical literature we have looked at, the book of Revelation has been the area that I have been the least enthusiastic to cover. There have been so many ideas formulated and different schemes assembled that I tremble to write even a few words about it. Nevertheless, it is part of the Word of God and it is our brief in this chapter to take a fleeting tour of the Bible, so that we will be prepared to leave no area untouched when we have our quiet times.

The title 'Revelation' comes from the Greek word meaning 'unveiling'. And the book itself is a letter originally composed to be circulated among the seven churches in Asia (featured in its first three chapters). These churches were under attack from outside and from within. And when the Lord Jesus speaks to them He exposes moral and spiritual compromise (Revelation 2:12-17, 20), a forsaking of the 'first love' of Christ (Revelation 2:1-7), spiritual deadness (Revelation 3:1-6) and tepid commitment (Revelation 3:14-22). Added to this there were also external pressures that came from earthly and spiritual powers (Revelation 2:9-10).

At the very beginning of the book John says 'blessed is he who reads and those who hear the words of this prophecy, and keep those things which are written in it' (1:3). And this serves to remind us that it has an important message to the seven churches. Revelation presents an unfolding drama, full of heady symbolism, startling visions and fantastic images. It comes to the triumphant conclusion that Christ will triumph, Satan will be crushed, and the church will overcome and reach the New Jerusalem. Nevertheless, while the emphasis is on the future, its victorious message is relevant for today. Revelation is an encouragement to all who face opposition and persecution. And as we witness the intensifying conflict between the church and the state, played out in the visions recounted by John, it challenges us to be overcomers, and it urges us to set our sights on the ascended Lord Jesus.

When our Bible reading plan takes us into Revelation there are a few basic principles that will help us steer a clear course through the book without getting side-tracked. First, we should reflect on the triumphant figure of the ascended Christ, who dominates the book. Secondly, we should link the drama unfolded before us to the seven churches to which it was originally written. Thirdly, the book should motivate us to take our eyes off the things of this world and prepare for the reality that is to come.

As promised this has been a brief orientation tour of the Bible. I trust that it has whetted our appetites and fuelled our enthusiasm so that we leave no area of our Bibles untouched.

Some footsteps to follow

A few years ago, I helped to lead a Christian Skiing holiday. The Instructor who taught the more advanced skiers used to take his class to the top of the mountain, begin to ski down and call out 'follow my tracks.' He was such a skilled skier that very few people could follow the neat trail that he had carved in the snow, but his class found this method very useful because it helped to lead them in the right direction. In this chapter, we are going to follow the tracks of some great men of God, three from the pages of the Bible, and three from the archives of history. We may not be as gifted and knowledgeable as they were, but their example can be a source of great inspiration and practical help. And to encourage us a little more, we will meet an ordinary young couple, who love the Lord and treasure their quiet times.

The perfect example

Whenever I read obituaries in the newspaper, I find it sobering to think that a person's life can be summarised in the space of a few columns of newsprint. Although the people who write these tributes are sensitive, thorough, and concise, they can be a little unbalanced. They have a tendency to emphasise people's achievements, exaggerate their strengths, hail their successes, and play down their weaknesses and failures. The Bible is very different, when it introduces us to the characters around which it is written it doesn't pretend that they are perfect, and it makes no attempt to hide their weaknesses. Not only does this remind us that 'all have sinned and fall short of the glory of God' (Romans 3:23), it also emphasises the fact that there is only one perfect example – the Lord Jesus Christ.

Every part of Jesus' life and character stands as an example to us (see Philippians 2:6-7, 1 Peter 2:21), particularly the way in which he set time aside to be alone with His Father. There are many such instances recorded in the Gospels. Immediately after He had fed the five thousand, Jesus sent the disciples away in a boat, dispersed the crowd and went onto a mountain to be alone with God (Matthew 14:22-23). Mark shows us how prayer was Jesus' first activity of the day when he tells us that 'in the morning, having risen a long while before daylight, He went out and departed to a solitary place; and there He prayed' (Mark 1:35). And Luke says that Jesus 'often withdrew into the wilderness and prayed' (Luke 5:16).

Unlike the Pharisees and Teachers of the law, the long periods Jesus spent in prayer were not part of a strict religious regime, they were fuelled by His relationship with His Father. This was a relationship based on love (John 5:20), built on intimacy (John 10:30) and expressed in Jesus' desire to please His Father (John 5:30).

Being the Son of God, Jesus had a unique relationship with His Father. However, the Bible tells us the Holy Spirit is at work within us renewing us into the likeness of Jesus (Colossians 3:10, 2 Corinthians 4:16). Our part in this process is to follow His example, and if we are going to do this it is vital that we make time to be alone with God and grow in our relationship with Him.

The Right mind-set

It would be an understatement to say that Paul, Silas and Timothy did not have a very easy time when they preached the Gospel in Thessalonica. Paul had visited the synagogue and addressed the Jews who were present 'explaining and demonstrating that the Christ had to suffer and rise again from the dead, and saying, "This Jesus whom I preach to you is the Christ." (Acts 17:3). The reception was mixed; there were a number of Jews and Greeks who responded to the Gospel, but the Jews set themselves up in opposition and organized a rabble of evil men who turned on Paul and Silas. They had whipped up such a storm that Paul was forced to leave Thessalonica under the cover of darkness.

The next port of call was a place called Berea, and the people encountered there were very different from the people who had opposed them at Thessolonica. They are described as 'fair minded' (Acts 17:11), the Greek word means that they were well disposed toward the truth, and they received the Word with complete willingness of mind. This was shown in the way that they 'searched the Scriptures daily' (Acts 17:11). American preacher, John MacArthur, contrasts this approach to the attitude that seems to be widespread in the today's Church. He says the Church 'has moved away from careful biblical thinking and has tolerated far too much shoddy teaching. Fewer and fewer Christians are approaching life with the Berean perspective. They haven't developed the habit of discerning or applying biblical principles to their daily situations.'[38] The Bereans set us an example, which urgently needs to be followed. We must 'search the Scriptures daily', put our minds to work and receive the Word, applying it to our everyday lives.

The man after God's heart

David's life might be called a classic 'rags to riches' story'; from the modest origins of a shepherd boy, he became one of the richest and most powerful men in the Middle East. He ruled Israel at the pinnacle of its power and prestige, owning palaces, treasures, land, and slaves; but whenever he spoke of his wealth he contrasted it with something that was far more precious to him – God's Word. 'I love your commandments more than gold, yes, than fine gold!' (Psalm 119:127), he said 'how precious also are your thoughts to me, how great is the sum of them' (Psalm 139:17). The Word of God was 'a lamp' to David's feet, and 'a light' for his path (Psalm 119:105). It enabled him to 'keep his way pure' (Psalm 119:9), it revived him (Psalm 119:25), and it was his meditation 'all the day' (Psalm 119:97).

Although David was rich and powerful, his life was not always easy. In the Psalms he speaks of enemies who surrounded him (Psalm 17:9), of dilemmas he struggled with (Psalm 25), and conspiracies that threatened to undermine his position (Psalm 31:13). There were times when David suffered as a consequence of his sin and had to face the Lord's chastening. That is why God had allowed David's son, Absalom, to conspire against him, drive him out of Jerusalem and abuse his concubines. In the course of this humiliating experience, David and the men who remained loyal to him encountered Shimei, a relative of Saul, who leapt at the opportunity to taunt him. Shimei approached David and unleashed a torrent of abuse, saying 'Come out! Come out! You bloodthirsty man, you rogue! 'The LORD has brought upon you all the blood of the house of Saul, in whose place you have reigned; and the LORD has delivered the kingdom into the hand of Absalom your son. So now you are caught in your own evil, because you are a bloodthirsty man!' (2 Samuel 16:7-8). While he was saying this he pelted David with stones, and this was all too much for Abishai, one of

David's loyal men. 'Why should this dead dog go and curse my lord the king?' He said. 'Please, let me go over and take off his head!' (2 Samuel 16:9). David would have none of this kind of talk, he urged Abishai to look to the Lord.

'And David said to Abishai and all his servants, 'See how my son who came from my own body seeks my life. How much more now may this Benjamite? Let him alone, and let him curse; for so the LORD has ordered him.' It may be that the LORD will look on my affliction, and that the LORD will repay me with good for his cursing this day' (2 Samuel 16:11-12).

To the echoes of Shimei's cursing, covered with dust and pelted with stones, David and his men continued to make their way along the road. Understandably, this experience was physically and emotionally draining, so they found a suitable place to stop and 'refreshed themselves there' (2 Samuel 16:14). While there would have been a lot of food to hand (see 2 Samuel 16:1) it is likely that David and his men did more than pitch camp, quench their thirst, satisfy their hunger and catch up with their sleep. 'Refreshed' means 'to take breath' or 'to sustain oneself', and it can also describe the soul. It is used to depict the rest that God took after the sixth day of creation (Exodus 31:17), and to speak of the 'longing soul' that God satisfies (Psalm 107:9). The refreshment that David and his men took would have had a spiritual dimension; they would have taken stock of their situation, looked to the Lord, and drawn strength from Him. On another occasion David and his men got back to their base to find that the Amalekites had taken their families captive. David's men were very distressed by this, held him responsible and threatened to stone him; but David 'strengthened himself in the LORD' (1 Samuel 30:6).

There were times when David seemed to be teetering on the brink of despair; in one Psalm he says his 'tears have been (his) food day and night' (Psalm 42:3), but he pulls himself back from the brink by directing his attention to the Lord.

'Why are you cast down, O my soul?
And why are you disquieted within me?

Hope in God, for I shall yet praise Him
For the help of His countenance.' (Psalm 42:5)

Stress and trauma are not unique to the day in which we live. David faced them too, but the Psalms show us that he would not let circumstances rule him. He would turn his problems to prayer, recall the mighty deeds of God (Psalm 143:5-6), and express this recollection in words of praise and declarations of hope. Although we cannot escape problems, stress and pressure, we shouldn't let them rule our lives; like David, we must thirst after God (Psalm 42:1), value His Word above everything else (Psalm 119:127, Psalm 19:10), and refresh ourselves in Him. The Devil really scores a point when we allow pressure and problems to affect our quiet times. It's at such times that we need them most!

A man who felt sorry for himself

James tells us that 'Elijah was a man with a nature like ours' (James 5:17), and never is this more evident than when we meet him tucked away in a cleft of Mount Horeb, on the run from Queen Jezebel. Psychologists would say that Elijah was suffering from 'post traumatic stress.' Buoyed up with a new-found confidence after his confrontation with the Prophets of Baal (1 Kings 18:20-40), Elijah heard some news that was to make quite an impact upon him. Queen Jezebel had sent him an intimidating message which said 'may the gods deal with me, be it ever so severely, if by this time tomorrow I do not make your life like that of one of them' (1 Kings 19:2). This had a very negative effect on Elijah and sent him running in the direction of Beersheba. Eventually he arrived, feeling exhausted, isolated, hungry, and very sorry for himself, and it was at this low point that God met with Him.

The first thing that God did for Elijah was to provide for his physical needs. Elijah was so depressed and dispirited, that he lay under a tree and asked God to bring his life to a swift conclusion. 'Now LORD, take my life, for I am no better than my fathers!' he said (1 Kings 19:4). God responded to this prayer, but not in the way that Elijah had anticipated; He provided food and sent an angel who told him to 'arise and eat' (1 Kings 19:7).

We will all go through phases when we find it very difficult to keep our quiet times going, and we may assume the problem to be spiritual when it is physical. Elijah's spirits were probably in the doldrums because he was drained from the confrontation at Mount Carmel, and this would have left him vulnerable to the effects of Jezebel's letter.

An Evangelist had been conducting a series of meetings at a University; at the end of the last meeting, one of the students who had been heavily involved spoke to him about some difficulties that were affecting his spiritual life. The Evangelist couldn't help noticing that this young man had heavy rings round his eyes. 'Can you try something for me?' he said. 'Of course', the student replied 'what do you want me to do?' He may have been expecting some deep spiritual counsel, but he was given a straight forward task; he was told to get an early night, have his quiet time the next morning, and then come and talk to the Evangelist. The next morning the student seemed to have a new lease of life. 'Thank you' he said with vibrancy in his voice, 'I feel so much better.' Like Elijah he thought his problem was spiritual instead of physical. As C.H. Spurgeon once observed: 'a mouthful of sea air, or a stiff walk in the wind's face, would not give grace to the soul, but it would yield oxygen to the body, which is next best.'39

After he had eaten his meal, and had caught up on his sleep, Elijah had another visit from the Angel of the LORD, this time he was given a word of re-direction. 'Arise and eat,' He said ' because the journey is too great for you' (1Kings 19:7).

When we meet with God, we have to be open to the things that He calls us to do. Having been conscious of a calling to the Ministry since my conversion, I went through a phase when I wanted to pursue my career, settle down, and put it right out of my mind. One day I sat down and opened my Bible at the chapter that I had reached in my daily meditation; it was Matthew 13, which contains the parable of the sower. In the course of my meditation, I came to identify the seed that Jesus spoke of as the calling that God had given to me. What had happened to it? It had suffered the same treatment as the seed that had fallen amongst the thorns; it had been choked by 'the cares of this world and the deceitfulness of riches' (Matthew 13:22). Looking back on that particular quiet time, I believe that it was one of the most significant that I have ever had, because I recommitted myself to the call that God had given me, and within eighteen months I had begun my training for the Ministry.

Chapter 8

Now that we have followed in the footsteps of some of the people we meet in God's Word, we'll move on to look at three men recorded in the archives of the history of the Church.

A man who battled with the bedclothes

On Saturday November 19th 1836, the city of Cambridge saw one of the most remarkable funerals ever to take place within its boundaries. The shops were shut, University lectures were cancelled, and the streets around Kings College thronged with people who had gathered to pay their final tribute to Charles Simeon. Simeon, a Fellow of Kings College and a Vicar of the Parish, had exercised such an effective ministry during his 44 years in Cambridge that at his death 'countless hearts felt that they had lost a father.'[40] He wasn't always such a gentle person; one of his biographers says that he had 'a hot temper and a forceful personality'[41] but humility 'was grafted in his heart by the mercy of God.'[42] Simeon was a man who grew in grace, and the secret of his spiritual growth lay in the way in which he 'had learned to walk in the Light where God is, and to have fellowship with Him'[43].

Between 1782 and 1812 Simeon lived in the Fellows building of Kings College. One of the main attractions of his lodgings was that he could easily climb from the attic onto the roof, where he could be alone with God. 'I shall now have a solitary oratory on the roof, where no eye but that of the Supreme can behold me'[44] he said. A close friend had commented that he once found Simeon 'so absorbed in the contemplation of the Son of God, and so overpowered with a display of His mercy to his soul, that he was incapable of pronouncing a single word.'[45]

Simeon resolutely set himself the goal of getting up early so that he could spend the first part of the day in the Word of God and in prayer. He didn't find this particularly easy, but he was determined to have his quiet time. As an inducement he decided that if he didn't manage to get up he would fine himself half a crown (which was a great deal of money in those days), and give it to his servant. Ingenious as this idea was, he soon accommodated his thinking. His servant was poor, he thought, she would find the gift of half a crown very useful, so it would be a good thing to lie in bed a little longer and help the poor lady. After this, he decided to follow a different strategy; every time that he failed to get out of bed to have his quiet time, he would throw a guinea into the water. He still struggled, and there was an occasion when he lost the battle, but he fulfilled his pledge.

A man who got to grips with God's Word

The journals of the great Evangelist of the 18th Century revival, George Whitefield, contain references to his 'stated hours of prayer.'[46] One of his constant companions during these hours was a set of Matthew Henry's Commentaries bought for the princely sum of £7, which was equivalent to 15 weeks of a labouring man's wages. Every morning, for two or three hours, Whitefield could be found on his knees poring over God's word and seeking God's face in prayer.

Whitefield was not a superficial reader; he would read a portion of scripture in the English and Greek, and then consider Matthew Henry's comments on the passage. After that, he would pray over every line of the passage until 'the passage in its essential message, had veritably become part of his soul.'[47]

A man who made God his pursuit

Two preachers took a walk in the woods, one of them stopped and sat on a log, while the other walked on a little further, knelt on a carpet of leaves and read his Bible. In the course of his meditation, God spoke to him and led him into an experience that was to make a mark on him for the rest of his life. 'All at once I saw God as I never saw him before,' he said. 'In that wooded sanctuary I fell on my face and worshipped. Since that experience, I have lost all interest in cheap religious thrills. The vacuous religious choruses we sing hold no attraction for me. I came face-to-face with the sovereign God, and since that time only God has mattered in my life.'[48] The name of that young man was Aiden Wilson Tozer, the great American preacher and writer who is universally known as a man who spent his life in the pursuit of God.

Tozer was deeply concerned about the spiritual shallowness that he saw in the Church and he attributed this to the lack of time that people spent with God. 'The dearth of great saints in this day' he said 'is due at least in part to our unwillingness to give sufficient time to the cultivation of the knowledge of God.'[49] Tozer said that the religious activities in which the Church immersed herself 'should be ordered in such a way as to leave plenty of time for the cultivation of the fruits of solitude and silence'[50]

Since his conversion, Tozer had shown a determination to spend time alone with God. In his younger days, this was not a particularly easy task; he lived in a house that was crammed with eight family members, and the numbers were often swelled by the presence of lodgers. The newly converted Tozer decided to take refuge in the basement of the house, using a small space behind the furnace to have his quiet times. He would be known to disappear for hours on end, which would be spent in his pursuit of God through prayer and meditation on the Word. His sister, Essie, recalled her first experiences of her brother's pursuit of God when she descended the stairs of the cellar and heard 'frightful groanings coming from the furnace.'[51] Thankfully, it didn't take her long to realise it was the sound of her brother, engaged in earnest prayer.

Prayer, Bible study, and Christian service were greatly valued by Tozer, but they were all subordinate to something he prized more than anything else, he described this as 'the inward habit of beholding God'[52]. This, for Tozer, was the foundation of the Christian life, but he believed it had fallen into neglect. 'We have almost forgotten that God is a person and as such can be cultivated as any person can,'[53] he wrote, adding that 'full knowledge of one personality by another cannot be achieved in one encounter. It is only after long and loving mental intercourse that the full possibilities of both can be explored.'[54]

Tozer's classic book, 'The Pursuit of God,' was written in the post war years, when the technical revolution was in its infancy. Even in those early days, he detected a change in the way that Christians were approaching their quiet times.

'A generation of Christians reared among push buttons and automatic machines is impatient of slower and less direct methods of reaching their goals. We have been trying to apply machine-age methods to our relationship with God. We read our chapter, have our short devotions and rush away, hoping to make up for our deep inward bankruptcy by attending another gospel meeting or listening to another thrilling story told by a religious adventurer lately returned from afar.'[55]

Those words first came into print in 1948, but they are even more relevant to this age of information technology. We need to make a conscious break with the thinking we have absorbed from our society, shun quick fixes, sensational experiences, and shallow spirituality and dedicate ourselves to the pursuit of God, making this the object of every quiet time.

People like us!

Jack and Lesley are young parents who live in the South of England. Jack holds down a demanding job and Lesley works 24 hours a day as a mother of their two young boys. As well as investing time in their own family, they are both involved in their local Church and Jack is part of the leadership team.

Both Jack and Lesley believe that the quiet time is a very important part of their Christian lives; 'You've got to keep up with your relationship with God,' says Jack, 'and you can't do that if you're not having your quiet times.' Jack gets up before the children are awake so that he can spend time with God. He begins with a short time of prayer, following the 'ACTS' formula (adoration – confession – thanksgiving – supplication), reads a passage of the Bible, reflects on it, and spends some time praying about it. Jack doesn't believe that the quiet time should be confined to the period he has set aside, he enthusiastically takes the passage or verses that have spoken to him into the day. His job has been very difficult and uncertain recently, and understandably this has had an effect on him, but during one of his quiet times he read Psalm 34:7: 'the angel of the LORD encamps all around those who fear Him, and delivers them.' This became a great source of encouragement to Jack, and it helped to get him through a very difficult day at work.

Lesley has her hands full looking after her family, and she has found it difficult to keep to a specific time. 'It's all right when you've got one child,' she says, 'you can have your quiet time when they're asleep, but when you've got two it's a lot more difficult.' However, Lesley is not one to give up easily, and throughout the day, she looks for five or ten-minute slots that she can 'snatch', she also reads some verses of the Bible before turning in for the night. 'I'd really love to have more time with the Lord' she says 'but the wonderful thing is that He really blesses me in the short periods that I have been able to grab.'

Chapter 8

Now that we have looked at the devotional lives of others, we should take encouragement from their struggles and draw lessons from their experiences. Let's remember one thing though, God doesn't want us to be another Whitefield or Tozer; He wants us to be ourselves!

'It's good to talk'

The place of prayer

It was six o 'clock on a Sunday evening, and I was due to preach in front of my fellow students within the hour. Nervously clutching my notes, I stumbled into the Minister's Vestry, I prayed with the Pastor of the Church, and I climbed the pulpit steps, launching myself into the service. Eventually the first part of my ordeal was over, but the worst was still to come – after the service, our Tutor was to lead us in a discussion in which the whole group would analyse the sermon I had preached. My Tutor began by expressing his thanks, and encouraging me with some positive comments about my sermon, and then he told me I had preached 'a standard evangelical sermon.' This put me at ease, but it proved to be a false sense of security, because he went on to say that a 'standard evangelical sermon' tells people they don't read their Bible or pray enough!'

Looking back on that nerve-racking evening I have never forgotten the lesson this taught me; it's not sufficient to tell people that they don't pray enough, every Christian is aware of that; it is much more effective to encourage people to have a greater appreciation of prayer.

Pinning prayer down

A person who is not a Christian would probably think of prayer as a religious act, but the Bible presents it as an essential part of a personal relationship with God. In the Old Testament, a combination of Hebrew words are put to use to portray prayer as a child-like dependence on a Sovereign God, who is all-powerful and deeply caring. The New Testament sharpens the focus, picturing prayer as a continual expression of a relationship with our Heavenly Father.

When I was the speaker on a Christian holiday, I shared a room with a man who was incredibly tidy. When I asked him how he managed this, he told me it was a matter of making sure that everything is put in its 'proper place'. We can import that kind of thinking into our quiet times; we can have worship, Bible reading and prayer neatly arranged in their 'proper places'. The problem with this approach is that it confines prayer to a single slot, when it should be woven into the fabric of the quiet time, and flow into the course of our everyday life. A letter, printed in the newspaper, written by a man describing himself as 'an ordained Minister who rides a motor bike', was a source of great encouragement to me. He was writing about the need to stop thinking of prayer as something that goes on within the four walls of a Church building, and to think of it as a part of one's everyday life. He said that sometimes he found it easier to pray and worship God when he was out on his bike, although he added that 'it is not a good idea to close your eyes in prayer or to lift your hands in praise' when you do this!

Principles for prayer

There have been so many books written about prayer that there is little I can add. This is a book about the quiet time, so we will use the rest of this chapter to think about some Biblical principles which will help us pray more effectively during the time that we set aside to meet with God.

Honest to God!

An old friend came to stay with me. We hadn't seen each other for a number of years, and he had never heard me preach. After the Sunday morning service, we had a cup of coffee together and, with familiar honesty, he told me what he thought of my preaching: 'Do you know that you put on a different voice when you preach?' he said. I knew what he meant; when I am out of the pulpit I lapse into my native accent, but when I preach I do my utmost to hide it. He was really telling me that I wasn't being myself. I wonder if you are like that when you pray. I don't mean that you put on another accent, I mean that you are not quite yourself when you speak to God. If you look through the Bible, you'll see that some of the most effective prayers come from the lips of people who were honest and open with God. Habakkuk's prophecy was born from the cry 'O Lord, how long shall I cry, And you will not hear?' (Habakkuk 1:2). And when Jesus prayed in the garden of Gethsemene He was so troubled that 'His sweat became like drops of blood' (Luke 22:44) and He prayed 'Father, if it is your will remove this cup from Me; nevertheless not My will but Yours be done'

(Luke 22:42). If these people could be honest with God, you can too; you don't need to put on an act, besides, it's pointless because He knows everything about you!

Dare to be disciplined

Discipline is not a popular word; to many, it sounds like legalism, but the two things are very different. Legalism describes the way some people try to establish a relationship with God by their own efforts. Discipline is a matter of making sure that our old nature doesn't get the better of us. It is best described by Paul, when he said 'I discipline my body and bring it into subjection, lest when I have preached to others, I myself should become disqualified' (1 Corinthians 9:27).

Some people can be fanatical about exercise; they drive themselves further every day and feel an overwhelming sense of failure if they don't meet their targets. That is legalism. Other people, realising the benefit they will gain, take their exercise whether they feel like it or not, without pushing themselves beyond their limitations. That is discipline.

When Paul wrote to the Christians in Galatia he said 'let us not become conceited, provoking one another, envying one another' (Galatians 5:26). 'Conceited' translates a word that describes the way one might talk things up, or exaggerate, and 'provoke' comes from a word that was used to describe a contest in the field of combat or athletics. They picture a church competing to see who can be the most 'spiritual.' Legalism often has its roots in someone's desire to prove themselves to be better than everyone else. Discipline originates from a love for the Lord and realism about our own weaknesses and shortcomings.

How do we exercise discipline? First, we mustn't depend on our feelings. There will be times when we are eager to pray, and there will be times when we are reluctant, but God's Word tells us to 'pray without ceasing' (1 Thessalonians 5:17).

Secondly, we need to assemble our thoughts. Most of us have minds that take us in all sorts of directions, so it is important to have some kind of list which will help us keep our thoughts on track. I have a little book in which I can make a note of the things that I need to pray about. It has a page for urgent needs, for my Church, my family, and my work. And when I come to the point in my quiet time when I pray for such things, I have the information readily at hand. While I find this a helpful tool, the Holy Spirit often leads me on an unexpected route, and I find myself praying for people or issues that I didn't expect .

Thirdly, we should use the Bible. God's Word is the most effective, but the most neglected resource that we have. When people come to me for advice about prayer, I invariably take them to the Bible. I encourage them to use the prayers that Paul presents at the beginning of some of his letters, or the Psalms, or some of the other great prayers in the Bible, not to mention the Lord's Prayer! When I pray for my Church, I often turn to the prayer that can be found at the beginning of Philippians:

'And this I pray, that your love may abound still more and more in knowledge and all discernment, that you may approve the things that are excellent, that you may be sincere and without offence till the day of Christ, being filled with the fruits of righteousness which are by Jesus Christ, to the glory and praise of God.'
(Philippians 1:9-11)

Initially I ask God that my love 'may abound still more and more in knowledge and all discernment' asking Him to show areas in my life that need to change in the light of these verses. I then pray for the members of my church, for their relationship with God, and their relationship with one another. After that I pray for their Christian lives, asking the Lord that they might be 'sincere and without offence.' And finally, I look forward to the day when they stand at the judgement seat of Christ, and pray that they might be 'filled with the fruits of righteousness.'

Remember reverence

It is wonderful to know that God is our Father and to be able to boldly come into His presence, but there must be a balance. I am very fond of quoting the verse in Hebrews that calls us to 'come boldly to the throne of grace' (Hebrews 4:16), but I am not always so keen to think about another verse: 'let us have grace that we may serve (worship) God acceptably with reverence and godly fear. For our God is a consuming fire' (Hebrews 12:28-29).

It is important that we balance boldness with reverence. Reverence, though, should not be understood as a cringing fear, but a loving realisation of the greatness of our God and the privilege that we, as His children, have been given in being able to approach Him.

Confess your sins

When leading a Communion Service, I usually read the relevant verses in 1 Corinthians 11 and, in view of the statement 'let a man examine himself' (28), I provide a few moments to give people the opportunity to examine their hearts and lives, and confess their sin to God. Although we don't want to put ourselves in a position where we become obsessed with the possibility that we might have sinned, we do need to be aware of our sins so that we can confess them to God and receive His forgiveness. David said 'if I regard iniquity in my heart the Lord will not hear' (Psalm 66:18), but John reminds us that 'if we confess our sins, He is faithful and just to forgive us our sins and to cleanse us from all unrighteousness' (1 John 1:9). God's Word has a way of exposing our sins, and when it does, we should confess them to Him, in the confidence that the blood of Christ cleanses us from all sin.

Open the box!

The Bible depicts prayer as an essential part of our relationship with God, so we should not put it in a box marked 'quiet time'; we must break the box open so it can filter into every corner of our lives. We can pray about a difficult piece of work that we have to do, we can send up an urgent prayer when we are faced with a dilemma or a difficult situation, we can call to God for help when a difficult colleague provokes us. If our lives are 'living sacrifices, holy and pleasing to God' (Romans 12:1 NIV) we will make sure that He is our constant reference point, and there is only one way to do that – to pray!

Things that go bump

Appraising the problems

After weeks and weeks of anticipation the summer holidays were just a few days in the distance, and the normal school timetable had broken down to make way for end of term activities. The school sports took place on a cloudless summer day, and the sun beat down on us as we sat with our parents waiting for our race to be called. Eventually it was my turn; I took my place, I looked towards the finishing post, and decided that I would win! After what seemed like an eternity, the starting gun finally went off, and I bolted into action and tore ahead of all the other boys. Little by little I became aware of a pain in my stomach; it started as a twinge, it grew to a stab, and it developed into a terrible ache. I felt as if an invisible hand had reached out and grabbed hold of something inside me, it was unbearable, and it seemed to be getting worse all the time. The pain had taken my mind from the race itself and had given the boys who were behind me an advantage; one by one, they passed me by, until I staggered to the finishing post, having come in last.

Years later, I discovered that athletes call this experience 'the pain barrier.' They tell me that there is a point in a race at which your body seems to conspire against you, stab you with pain, and try and stop you from maintaining the speed that you have built up. The key to overcoming this is to keep up a steady pace, reserve some energy for the end of the race, and keep your sights set on the finishing post. Many of us have faced similar problems with our quiet times; we have started off well, we have been driven by a determination to give God the very best, but difficulties have thrown us off course. This chapter contains some good news; we can break through the 'pain barrier', overcome our problems, and get our quiet times back to a steady pace. But we must begin by facing up to them.

Common questions
I have talked to many people about their quiet times; here are some of the questions that I am asked with the most frequency.

How long should my quiet time be?

Before I went to Bible College, my employers sent me on a part time course in business and finance. After studying for 'A' level it had been ingrained into me that a piece of work had to be a specified length, so, when I was handed my first study assignment, I asked the lecturer how long my piece of work should be. 'I don't know, Simon,' he replied with a mischievous look on his face 'how long is a piece of string?' I must have looked a little confused, because he went on to explain that, rather than thinking of my work in terms of a sheet of paper that needed to be filled, I should see it as a task to be completed.

In Chapter 4, we considered the danger of seeing our quiet time as a period of time that needed to be filled, and this question uncovers the same danger. The person who spends thirty minutes in his or her quiet time is not necessarily closer to God than the person who spends twenty minutes. Set aside the amount of time that will be comfortable for you to worship God, to read His Word and to spend time in prayer without rushing. If you find you finish earlier than expected, don't worry, you may have read the passage more quickly, absorbed the lesson more readily, or gathered your thoughts more efficiently. Remember the one who is watching the clock is you – not God!

Should there be a structure to my Quiet Times?

Structure can be a helpful tool, but if we're not careful, it can become a hard taskmaster that robs us of the joy and vitality of a quiet time.

A structure can help us to channel our thoughts and make the most of the time we have set aside, but we mustn't be afraid to vary it, change it or even disregard it.

I find it helpful to follow a Bible reading plan, read the passage that has been set for the particular day, spend a little time thinking about it, and then turn it into prayer. These prayers centre on the passage that I have been reading and involve worship, confession of sin, thanksgiving and specific requests. After this, I move on to a more general time of prayer, when I bring the needs of my Church, friends, and family to God. Although I find this pattern very useful, there are times when I vary it so that I don't get stuck in one particular routine. We need a pattern to follow, and it must be the one that suits us best, but we shouldn't be afraid of variety.

Should my Quiet Times develop?

The quiet time is the nerve centre of the Christian life, and as such, it is part of the process by which we grow, but not the whole process. We will also grow through trials (James 1:2-3), fellowship with other Christians (Hebrews 10:24-25), teaching (2 Timothy 1:13) and witness (Philemon 6). As we progress in the Christian life, we will probably find that the basic composition of our quiet time stays the same while our intimacy with God deepens.

COMMON PROBLEMS

Dry Patches

The first few months of my Christian life were wonderful. I was fuelled by a new purpose in life, filled with a joy that I'd never known before and fulfilled by a peace 'that passes all understanding' (Philippians 4:7). Suddenly, it all seemed to go dry. 'I can't understand it,' I thought to myself, 'I am a child of God, I shouldn't be feeling this way.' I was so disturbed by this that I went to talk to an older Christian who was able to give me some good advice. He told me that after the Lord Jesus was filled with the Holy Spirit He was led into the wilderness (Luke 4:1). 'It's quite normal for you to feel this way,' he said 'we all have to face wilderness experiences, and this is what is happening to you.' That particular dry patch lasted for about six weeks, but looking back over the years, I can identify many such experiences. The key to getting to the other side of them is to know how to keep going. How is that possible?

First, we mustn't rely on our feelings. Although the Christian life is full of soaring joys, there will be times of sadness. Paul looks back on one of the lowest points in his Christian life and tells us that he and his companions were 'burdened beyond measure, above strength, so that we despaired even of life' (2 Corinthians 1:8). David called out to God in prayer and said 'O my God, my soul is cast down within me' (Psalm 42:6). Neither Paul nor David let their feelings rule them. David gave himself a good talking to, saying 'why are you cast down, O my soul? And why are you disquieted within me? Hope in God, for I shall yet praise Him for the help of His countenance' (Psalm 42:11). And Paul goes on to say 'we had the sentence of death in ourselves, that we should not trust in ourselves but in God who raises the dead' (2 Corinthians 1:9). Both men acknowledged their feelings but refused to be ruled by them.

Secondly, we need some self-discipline. It is relatively easy to have a quiet time when things are going well, but the test will come during the dry patches, and discipline will help to pull us through.

Thirdly, we shouldn't be afraid to change the pattern we have been following. When I experienced my first 'dry patch', a friend, who had been a Christian longer than me, suggested that I break out of my normal pattern. When I followed his advice my quiet times were given a new lease of life. That's why I have provided a sample of some of the different approaches that can be taken, in chapter 5.

Finally, we must not bear it alone. We should ask a close Christian friend to pray for us. After all, the Bible calls us to 'bear one another's burdens, and so fulfil the law of Christ.' (Galatians 6:2).

Meandering minds

The moment that I begin my quiet time, I am aware of all sorts of distracting thoughts swimming around my mind, and I have tried to trace their source. It is possible that I am the kind of person who is easily distracted. A more likely explanation, however, is that, having been buried in my mind, the quiet time provides these thoughts with an opportunity to emerge.

Instead of fighting off distracting thoughts, we might find it more effective if we let them emerge and spend a moment separating trivia from things that need to be given attention. Having done this, we should note them down, put the list to one side, and get on with our quiet time. If a thought continues to intrude, we can bring the matter to the Lord and leave it in His hands.

Now that we have dealt with the thoughts that distract us, we can begin to train our minds to concentrate on the Word of God. As a boy, I had a dog that I used to take for a walk. He seemed to have an inborn tendency to wander off, but little by little I trained him. This was my first lesson in realism; for most of the time he was obedient, but occasionally his urge to wander got the better of him. I had to accept that I could restrain him, but I couldn't change him. We have got to be realistic about our wandering minds; we can train them, we can increase our concentration, but we will fight a constant battle with stray thoughts. Let's remember that it is a problem – not a sin, otherwise we'll burden ourselves with a misplaced sense of guilt.

High days and holidays

After months of hard work, the long haul to your annual holiday has finally arrived. At last you can re-charge your batteries, renew your sanity, and enjoy the luxury of having time on your hands. The first day seems to go to plan; you have a little longer in bed than normal, a refreshing quiet time followed by a hearty breakfast, before you enjoy the day's recreation. On the second day, you find that a few obstacles stand in the way of your quiet time – but you overcome them. However, by the fourth day, your determination seems to have dissolved into a sea of apathy. You return from your holiday physically and mentally refreshed, but spiritually drained and deeply disappointed.

This is a common experience; we all begin our holidays with great expectations of leisurely quiet times, not to mention catching up on the reading that we've been intending to do! In reality, when our holidays come, we fit so snugly into a slow pace of life, we neglect the very things that were in the forefront of our minds as we set off for our holiday. What is the best approach to take?

We should start by being realistic; holidays are times when we relax, and relaxation slows us down. Rather than entertain great ambitions that will lead to disappointment, it is better to set some realistic goals, and establish a steady pace which will run the course.

In the early years of my ministry, I was involved with a Christian organisation that provided holidays for young people. At the first training weekend I attended, I heard about the excursions and activities organised as part of the holidays. When the time for questions came, I asked if leaders were allowed to go on them and the man who had been addressing us stifled a polite laugh; 'Of course you can' he said 'we want you to enjoy yourself!' Over the years I was involved in leading many of these holidays, and I found it a great blessing to be part of a group of

Christians who knew how to enjoy themselves in a way that was honouring to the Lord. Don't divorce the things that you enjoy about your holiday from your relationship with God – they come from Him. I often think of the way that the Psalmist said 'whom have I in heaven but you? And there is none upon earth that I desire besides you'(Psalm 73:25). All that we enjoy on our holidays is a gift from God, and if we spend a moment giving thanks for these things, everything will be put into perspective.

Complex problems

As we think about more complicated problems we have to be aware of the danger of oversimplifying the possible solutions. The very nature of these difficulties caution us that, in the limitations of this chapter, we can only begin to grapple with them.

Depression

We all have times when we are low, but some are unfortunate enough to suffer severe depression. There are many people in the Bible who went through the same thing. David talks about the way in which his soul was 'cast down' (Psalm 42:6). Elijah was so despondent that he wanted to die (1 Kings 19:4). And there was a point when the despair experienced by Paul and his fellow workers was so crushing that they felt as if they had been given the death sentence (2 Corinthians 1:9).

In his classic book 'Spiritual Depression', Martin Lloyd Jones tells us that 'the main art in spiritual living is to know how to handle yourself.'[56] To tackle this problem we will have to be realistic about the effects of depression and develop some tactics that will help us to fight back.

Depression often affects the concentration, and if you find this a difficulty, you mustn't load yourself down with guilt. Rather than try to keep to the pattern that you're used to, it might be more effective to spend a shorter period of time on something that you find more accessible. Someone who has struggled with depression told me that a 'Daily Light' had been a 'real lifeline' to her, because it provided a short selection of texts that were suited to her attention span. If your condition has left you feeling numbed and unloved, turn to the relevant parts of the Bible that remind you of God's love. Try taking encouragement from Romans 8:28: 'all things work together for good to those who love God, who are the called according to His purpose' And draw comfort from Jesus' words: 'Let not your heart be troubled; you believe in God, believe also in Me. In My Father's house are many mansions; if it were not so I would have told you. I go to prepare a place for you' (John 14:1-2).

Everyone has a tendency to wear a mask that disguises his or her true feelings, but there is no need to do that when we come before God. When we are in the depths of depression, we have the release of being able to speak to the Lord with complete honesty in the awareness that He knows everything about us. The Prophet Jeremiah had moments when he was tortured by the misery brought upon him by persecution; in the depths of his despondency, he spoke to God with complete and utter honesty:

' O LORD, You induced me, and I was persuaded;
You are stronger than I, and have prevailed.
I am in derision daily;
Everyone mocks me.
For when I spoke, I cried out;
I shouted, "Violence and plunder!"
Because the word of the LORD was made to me
A reproach and a derision daily.
Then I said, "I will not make mention of Him,
Nor speak anymore in His name."
But His word was in my heart like a burning fire
Shut up in my bones;
I was weary of holding it back,
And I could not. (Jeremiah 20:7-9)

Although we must never minimise the anguish brought by depression, we ought to be careful that we don't make it the focal point of our quiet times. When I spent a little time browsing the Internet, I came across some advertisements for Bible software that had been designed for Christians who suffer with depression. One of the products on offer was a Bible programme that was promoted as 'the only Bible Software specifically written for people in recovery'. If you don't own a Computer you can purchase Bibles which 'help you improve your present relationship with God to heal the hurts of the past.'[57] I have great misgivings about these kinds of Bibles, because they imply that people who suffer with depression are different from other Christians and therefore need a different kind of Bible.

When my Pastor counselled people who were in the grip of depression, he used to remind them that, instead of striving, they should 'hold themselves in place, and rest in the Lord'. Those words are a beautiful reminder that, when suffering depression, we should be ourselves and rest in the God who loves us.

Bereavement

The Book of Common Prayer tells us that 'even in life we are in the midst of death', and it is a sobering fact that everyone reading this book will face periods of bereavement. In view of this, it is important that the quiet time becomes an established and natural part of our lives so that, when bereavement comes, God can bring to mind scriptures that have already become woven into the fabric of our lives.

A lady who had suffered a devastating loss told me that the immediate effect of her bereavement, together with the practical arrangements needing to be made, put her on 'auto pilot', and this is a common experience. Many people find that, in the weeks that immediately follow their loss, they are caught up in all the activity of preparations for the funeral and settling their loved one's affairs. After this initial period ends, they find themselves going through the motions of everyday life without consciously taking anything in. This is part of the bereavement process, and we must understand that God knows everything about us and can speak to us in this situation.

Other people find that the loss of a loved one makes them numb. They can't concentrate, they don't know what they are doing, and they can't get on with things they would like to do. This makes it extremely difficult to follow the pattern of a quiet time they are used to, but it may help them to follow through verses that speak to their condition. Scripture Gift Mission have produced some excellent booklets that select such verses, and Gideon

Bibles also provide a very useful section containing Bible references designed to help people as they struggle with the range of emotions unleashed on them during the bereavement process.

As members of God's family, we have a responsibility to comfort people who have lost a loved one, but it is vital that we do this with gentleness and sensitivity. We must be careful not to cross the line between encouragement and pressure, if the words we choose make people feel pressured into prayer and Bible reading. It will only result in guilt if they find they cannot get down to it. We should assure them that short anguished prayer is quite normal during the bereavement process.

Above all, we should not see grief as an intrusion into our quiet times. The loss of a loved one takes us on an emotional roller coaster which will haul us through bouts of denial, anger, guilt, anxiety, depression, doubt, sorrow, numbness, self pity, and regret. The anguished and sometimes angry cries of the Psalmist show us that we do not have to withhold these emotions when we speak to God. Indeed, it is important to put them into words, because 'there is not a word on my tongue, but behold O Lord, you know it altogether' (Psalm 139: 4). There will be times when we feel the urge to express anger that we feel. Should we resist this, compose ourselves, and put on a more compliant face when we come to God? Not if we follow the Psalmists example!

'But to You I have cried out, O LORD,
And in the morning my prayer comes before You.
LORD, why do You cast off my soul?
Why do You hide Your face from me?
I have been afflicted and ready to die from my youth;
I suffer Your terrors;
I am distraught.
Your fierce wrath has gone over me;
Your terrors have cut me off.
They came around me all day long like water;
They engulfed me altogether.
Loved one and friend You have put far from me,
And my acquaintances into darkness.' (Psalm 88:13-18)

It will take time for a person who has lost a loved one to reach the point where they are able to let go and pick up the threads of their life. Our responsibility is to give them support and to show patience. A lady has been kind enough to write down some of her thoughts about a loss that she suffered a few years ago, and her words give hope to everyone reading this book who is conscious of an aching loss in their life.

'In time God does help us to overcome the turmoil and brings His peace and assurance to the situation. Prayer becomes even more precious; His Word becomes a stronghold. The realisation dawns that He had been there all along, even in the darkest moments.'[58]

Doubt

It was the end of a busy day at the office. I had answered my last telephone call and packed away my files. 'Did you see that programme called 'Jesus the Evidence' last night?' a colleague asked. The programme he spoke about attempted to put discredited theories about the identity of Jesus into a popular format and concluded that the 'Jesus of the Gospels' contrasts with 'the Jesus of history.' I had seen the programme and had expected to be asked about it, so I told him that I had watched it and I pointed out the areas where it had its facts wrong. Someone else in the office overheard our discussion and decided to join in, forming a two pronged attack against my rigorous defence of the Gospels. While it was all done in good humour, this brief conversation turned into a severe grilling during which I was bombarded with question after question. After about forty minutes intense debate, we agreed to disagree, and I was finally able to leave the office. On my journey home I felt mentally and spiritually drained, and all sorts of uncomfortable questions seemed to be wriggling around in my mind. 'What if these people are right?' 'What if the Gospels aren't true?' 'What if I'm not following a risen Saviour?' Thankfully, they were soon dispelled and the Lord gave me a wonderful sense of His presence, but that experience made me realise the effect that a sceptical society can have on us, and one consequence may be that doubts will occasionally intrude into our quiet times.

We can begin to tackle the problem by defining the doubt that is going through our mind. In the course of our Christian lives, we will struggle with different forms of doubt. The most common are emotional doubts – 'does God love me?'—and intellectual doubt – 'is this really true?' When things go wrong we may wrestle with circumstantial doubt—'why has God let me down?'—although this often comes from a lack of trust rather than scepticism. And when we react against something that the Bible tells us to do, we may even entertain sinful doubt—'does it really mean this?'

It might seem as if a doubt has just come into your mind, but the likelihood is that its origins lay elsewhere. It may relate to something that has happened to you, in which case you will need to work it through in prayer and come to a position of trust. It might have been prompted by a genuine question, or a broader intellectual problem you have, and in this case, you will need to do some serious thinking, or talk it through with another Christian.

Our psychological make-up can also be at the root of doubts. We may go through periods when we doubt God's love for us because we are insecure, or we may struggle with a statement that we have read in the Bible because we are the kind of person who likes to see every side of the argument. Gideon seems to display this characteristic after the Angel of the Lord met him and told him that he had been chosen to deliver his people from the Midianites. He responded to this exciting news by asking how he could save his people when he was the lowest member of the lowest clan in Israel. 'Surely I will be with you, and you shall defeat the Midianites as one man' the Lord replies (Judges 6:16). That was not enough for Gideon and he asked for a sign. The sign came when a young goat and some unleavened bread, which had been prepared as a sacrifice, were consumed by fire when the Angel of the Lord touched them with the end of His staff. A little later Gideon crept out, under the cover of night, and destroyed the altars erected in honour of Baal. After he had taken this bold step, he seemed to have another tinge of uncertainty:

'Gideon said to God, "If You will save Israel by my hand as You have said — look, I shall put a fleece of wool on the threshing floor; if there is dew on the fleece only, and it is dry on all the ground, then I shall know that You will save Israel by my hand, as You have said." And it was so. When he rose early the next morning and squeezed the fleece together, he wrung the dew out of the fleece, a bowlful of water'. (Judges 6:36-38).

This still does not seem to have been enough, so he asked for one more sign:

'Then Gideon said to God, "Do not be angry with me, but let me speak just once more: Let me test, I pray, just once more with the fleece; let it now be dry only on the fleece, but on all the ground let there be dew." And God did so that night. It was dry on the fleece only, but there was dew on all the ground'. (Judges 6:39-40)'.

Some people love puzzles, they look on them as an opportunity to stretch their minds. Others consider them sheer hard work. These different approaches mirror the way that we can tackle doubts; we can see them as a challenge that will help us to develop our thinking and strengthen our faith, or we can see them as an obstacle that we cannot overcome. It is the former who rise to the challenge, and the latter who fall flat on their faces.

Serious illness

Illness can be a huge drain on our physical and mental resources, and we shouldn't be surprised that it has an effect on our quiet times. If recovery involves a long period in hospital, this problem is aggravated by the distractions of a busy hospital ward.

If you face a period in hospital, take a devotional book with you. The book shouldn't be too difficult or mentally taxing, but it should be biblical and practical. I would recommend 'Daily Light', which contains a daily selection of verses around a chosen theme, and 'Drawing Near', by John MacArthur, which provides a short, substantial thought on a verse of Scripture for each day of the year, together with suggestions for prayer.

Lack of privacy on hospital wards can present a problem, but if you have a Bible or a devotional book on your bedside cabinet, most staff and patients will not interrupt you when you are reading them. Praying aloud will be difficult, but you can overcome this by shutting everything else out and praying in the quietness of your own mind.

Don't forget that you are suffering from an illness, so you shouldn't expect too much of yourself. I often encourage people suffering in this way to read Psalm 139, where David declares 'O Lord, you have searched me and known me … Such knowledge is too wonderful for me; It is high, I cannot attain it' (Psalm 139:1,6). God's knowledge is perfect, He knows more about your illness than your Doctor, and He understands the effect it has on you; you must rest in Him. One person told me that when she came to this realisation, she began to see the whole of her stay in hospital as a quiet time, because she felt that she could 'keep in contact with God.'

You always look forward to the news that you can return home from hospital, but after the initial elation has worn away, it will not be long before you discover your limitations. Remember that you are still recovering, and you will not be able to follow the routine you have been used to. It may be useful to continue with the pattern of quiet times you followed when you were in hospital, and gradually change them as your health improves.

Visual disability

Unless the contents of this book are being read aloud or have been recorded on to tape, I don't anticipate that people with visual disability will be reading this. I have included this section so that those of us who can see will be able give practical help to those who are unable to do so.

If you have a friend who cannot see, make sure they have access to a recording of the Bible, and remember they are not able to get to the verses that they want to read as easily as you can. Spend time reading these verses to them and find their place on the tapes that they use. How about recording the verses that have been a great help to you so your friend has easier access to them?

Visually disabled people have told me that, because they rely on sound, ordinary household noises can be very distracting to them. A ride to a quiet place where they can be left for a little while would be very welcome.

Principles for Persistence

There is a lovely story about a father and his newly converted son. 'Dad I'm scared of something' said the young boy. 'Tell me what it is son and we can pray about it together.' 'Well,' he stammered, struggling to put his feelings into words, 'I'm scared I might slip away from God.' His father smiled, stretched out his hand, and told his son to put his hand inside, then he clenched it in a grip. 'Try and pull away from me' he said. Try as he might, the young boy could not release himself from his father's grip. 'My grip is stronger than yours,' said the father, 'and God's hold of you, is firmer than your hold of God!'

When we experience difficulties with our quiet times, we can persist in the confidence that God has a firmer hold on us than we have of Him. The Old Testament tells us that God loved us with 'an everlasting love' (Jeremiah 31:3). In the New Testament, Paul says 'God demonstrates His own love toward us, in that while we were still sinners, Christ died for us' (Romans 5:8), and Jude tells us that our responsibility is to keep ourselves 'in the love of God' (Jude 21). When the going gets tough, and the Christian life gets dry, we can encourage ourselves with the realisation that God loves us, and is more eager to meet with us than we are to meet with Him. What an incentive to set aside part of the day **for the worship of God, for the reading of the Word of God and for fellowship with God!**

Notes

1   **Richards, Lawrence O.,** Expository Dictionary of Bible Words: Zondervan, , Grand Rapids Michigan 1985 page 116

2   ibid.

3   **Hallesby, O,** Prayer, IVP, Leicester 1971 page 111

4   **Blanchard, John,** 'Truth for Life', Evangelical Press, Darlington, 1986 page 80

5   **Moo, Douglas J,** Tyndale Commentary on James, IVP, Leicester 1988, page 80

6   **Reinecker, Fritz** and **Rogers, Cleon,** Linguistic Key to the Greek New Testament, Zondervan, Grand Rapids, Michigan 1980, page 725

7   **Snyder, James L.,** 'In Pursuit of God', Christian Publications , Camp Hill, PA, 1991, page 10

8   IVP, Leicester

9   IVP, Leicester

10 Evangelical Press, Darlington

11 IVP, Leicester

12 Banner of Truth, Edinburgh

13 IVP, Leicester

14 Baker, Grand Rapids, Michigan

15 **Horton, Michael,** 'In the face of God', Word Publishing, Dallas, 1997, Page 158

16 **Morris, Leon,** 'Expository Reflections on the Letter to the Ephesians', Baker, Grand Rapids, Michigan, page 14

17 **Stott, John,** 'The Message of Ephesians', IVP, Leicester 1979

18 **Hallesby, O,** 'Prayer, IVP, Leicester 1971, page 178-179

19 Published by OM Books, Carlisle

20 Published by Banner of Truth, Edinburgh, also available in a daily format through Evangelical Press, Darlington

21 Published by Macdonald,Mclean, Virginia

22 Published by Crossways, Wheaton Illinois

23 See **Lloyd Jones, Martyn,** 'Spiritual Depression', Pickering and Inglis, London, 1981, page 20

24 **Green, Michael** Tyndale New Testament Commentary on 2 Peter and Jude, IVP Leicester, 1983 page 91

25 2 Corinthians 6:14

26 Grudem Wayne, Systematic Theology, Zondervan, Grand Rapids, Michigan, page 515

27 ibid

28 **Edwards, Brian H.,** The Ten Commandments for Today, Day One Publications, Epsom, Surrey, 1997 page 16

29 **Lloyd Jones, Martyn,** Studies in the Sermon on The Mount, IVP, Leicester 1976, page 199

30 **Goldsworthy, Graham,** 'Gospel and Kingdom', Lancer, Homebush West, NSW, Australia page 78

31 **Calvin, John,** preface to commentary on the Psalms Baker, Grand Rapids, Michigan, 1984 page 26

32 **Henry, Matthew,** 'A Commentary on the Whole Bible' Word Bible Publishers, Dallas, volume3 page 237

33 **Kidner, Derek,** 'Wisdom to Live By' IVP, Leicester 1985 page 11

34 For more help on the book of Job read 'Why Lord? The book of Job for today' by **Gary Benfold,** published by Day One Publications, Epsom, Surrey.

35 i.e Joshua, Judges, 1 and 2 Samuel, 1 and 2 Kings, 1 and 2 Chronicles, Ezra and Nehemiah

36 I am grateful to the 'Read Mark Learn' notes that have been produced by St. Helen's Church Bishopsgate.

37 Machen J. Grecham, The New Testament, Banner of Truth, Edinburgh1976, page 54

38 **MacArthur, John, Jr,** 'Our Sufficiency in Christ, page 130. Word Books, Dallas, 1991

39 **Spurgeon, C.H.,** Lectures to my students, Marshall Pickering, London, 1989 page 158

40 Moule H.G.C, Charles Simeon, IVP, Leicester 1956, page 178

41 op cit. page xii

42 ibid.

43 ibid.

44 op cit., page 133

45 op cit., page 135

46 **Dallimore, Arnold,** in 'George Whitefield' Banner of Truth, Edinburgh, 1970, page 81

47 **Dallimore, Arnold,** George Whitefield' Banner of Truth, Edinburgh 1970 , page 83

48 **Snyder, James L.,** 'In pursuit of God' Christian Publications, Camp Hill, PA, 1991 page 161

49 op cit. page 6

50 op cit. page 7

51 op cit. page 38

52 **Tozer, A.W.,** 'The Pursuit of God', STL, Carlisle, 1984 page 96

53 op cit. page 13

54 ibid

55 op cit. page 69

56 **Lloyd Jones, D.Martyn,** Spiritual Depression Pickering and Inglis, London, 1981 page 21

57 From Christian Book Distributors 1998 Bible Catalogue, page32

58 Reproduced with permission

YEAR

1

This Bible
reading plan
can be
started at any
point in the
year. It is not
dated so if
your readings
fall behind,
you can
recommence
them without
feeling that
you need to
catch up.

OLD TESTAMENT		NEW TESTAMENT	
1.	Genesis 1	1.	Matthew 1
2.	Genesis 2	2.	Matthew 2
3.	Genesis 3	3.	Matthew 3
4.	Genesis 4 ,5	4.	Matthew 4
5.	Genesis 6	5.	Matthew 5:1-26
6.	Genesis 7	6.	Matthew 5.27-48
7.	Genesis 8	7.	Matthew 6:1-18
8.	Genesis 9, 10	8.	Matthew 6:19-34
9.	Genesis 11	9.	Matthew 7
10.	Genesis 12	10.	Matthew 8.1-17
11.	Genesis 13	11.	Matthew 8: 18-34
12.	Genesis 14,15	12.	Matthew 9: 1-17
13.	Genesis 16	13.	Matthew 9:18-38
14.	Genesis 17	14.	Matthew 10: 1-20
15.	Genesis 18	15.	Matthew 10:21-42
16.	Genesis 19, 20	16.	Matthew 11
17.	Genesis 21,22	17.	Matthew 12: 1-23
18.	Genesis 23	18.	Matthew 12: 24-50
19.	Genesis 24	19.	Matthew 13: 1-30
20.	Genesis 25	20.	Matthew 13:31-58
21.	Genesis 26	21.	Matthew 14:1-21
22.	Genesis 27	22.	Matthew 14:22-36
23.	Genesis 28	23.	Matthew 15: 1-21
24.	Genesis 29, 30	24.	Matthew 15: 22-39
25.	Genesis 31	25.	Matthew 16
26.	Genesis 32	26.	Matthew 17
27.	Genesis 33	27.	Matthew 18:1-20
28.	Genesis 34, 35	28.	Matthew 18: 21-35
29.	Genesis 36	29.	Matthew 19
30.	Genesis 37	30.	Matthew 20:1-16
31.	Genesis 38, 39	31.	Matthew 20:17-34
32.	Genesis 40, 41	32.	Matthew 21: 1-22
33.	Genesis 42	33.	Matthew 21:23-46
34.	Genesis 43	34.	Matthew 22:1-22

YEAR 1

'What is a quiet time? It is not a religious ritual but a revolutionary opportunity'

	OLD TESTAMENT		NEW TESTAMENT
35.	Genesis 44	35.	Matthew 22:23-46
36.	Genesis 45, 46	36.	Matthew23:1-22
37.	Genesis 47	37.	Matthew 23:23-39
38.	Genesis 48	38.	Matthew 24:1-28
39.	Genesis 49, 50	39.	Matthew 24:29-51
40.	Psalm 1, 2	40.	Matthew 25:1-30
41.	Psalm 3, 4	41.	Matthew 25:31-46
42.	Exodus 1	42.	Matthew 26:1-25
43.	Exodus 2	43.	Matthew 26: 26-50
44.	Exodus 3	44.	Matthew 26: 51-75
45.	Exodus 4, 5	45.	Matthew 27: 1-26
46.	Exodus 6, 7	46.	Matthew 27:27-50
47.	Exodus 8	47.	Matthew 27: 51-66
48.	Exodus 9	48.	Matthew 28
49.	Exodus 10	49.	Acts 1
50.	Exodus 11, 12	50.	Acts 2: 1-21
51.	Exodus 13	51.	Acts 2: 22-47
52.	Exodus 14	52.	Acts 3
53.	Exodus 15	53.	Acts 4:1-22
54.	Exodus 16, 17	54.	Acts 4:23-37
55.	Exodus 18	55.	Acts 5:1-21
56.	Exodus 19	56.	Acts 5: 22-42
57.	Exodus 20	57.	Acts 6
58.	Exodus 21, 22	58.	Acts 7:1-21
59.	Exodus 23	59.	Acts 7:22-43
60.	Exodus 24, 25	60.	Acts 7: 44-60
61.	Exodus 26	61.	Acts 8:1-25
62.	Exodus 27	62.	Acts 8:26-40
63.	Exodus 28, 29	63.	Acts 9:1-21
64.	Exodus 30	64.	Acts 9: 22-43
65.	Exodus 31	65.	Acts 10: 1-23
66.	Exodus 32	66.	Acts 10: 24-48
67.	Exodus 33, 34	67.	Acts 11
68.	Exodus 35	68.	Acts 12

YEAR

1

'What is a quiet time? It is a part of the day that we set aside for the worship of God, for the reading of the Word of God and for fellowship with God.'

OLD TESTAMENT		NEW TESTAMENT	
69.	Exodus 36	69.	Acts 13:1-25
70.	Exodus 37,38	70.	Acts 13:26-52
71.	Exodus 39,40	71.	Acts 14
72.	Psalm 5, 6	72.	Acts 15:1-21
73.	Psalm 7, 8	73.	Acts 15: 22-41
74.	Leviticus 1	74.	Acts 16:1-21
75.	Leviticus 2	75.	Acts 16: 22-40
76.	Leviticus 3	76.	Acts 17:1-15
77.	Leviticus 4, 5	77.	Acts 17: 16-34
78.	Leviticus 6	78.	Acts 18
79.	Leviticus 7	79.	Acts 19:1-20
80.	Leviticus 8	80.	Acts 19: 21-41
81.	Leviticus 9, 10	81.	Acts 20:1-16
82.	Leviticus 11	82.	Acts 20:17-38
83.	Leviticus 12	83.	Acts 21: 1-17
84.	Leviticus 13	84.	Acts 21:18-40
85.	Leviticus 14 ,15	85.	Acts 22
86.	Leviticus 16	86.	Acts 23:1-15
87.	Leviticus 17	87.	Acts 23:16-35
88.	Leviticus 18	88.	Acts 24
89.	Leviticus 19, 20	89.	Acts 25
90.	Leviticus 21	90.	Acts 26
91.	Leviticus 22	91.	Acts 27:1-26
92.	Leviticus 23	92.	Acts 27:27-44
93.	Leviticus 24	93.	Acts 28
94.	Leviticus 25, 26	94.	Mark 1:1-22
95.	Leviticus 27	95.	Mark 1:23-45
96.	Psalm 9, 10	96.	Mark 2
97.	Psalm 11, 12	97.	Mark 3:1-19
98.	Numbers 1	98.	Mark 3: 20-35
99.	Numbers 2	99.	Mark 4:1-20
100.	Numbers 3	100.	Mark 4:21-41
101.	Numbers 4, 5	101.	Mark5:1-20
102.	Numbers 6	102.	Mark 5:21-43

YEAR 1

'Listening to God involves us understanding the meaning of the passage that we are reading, perceiving what God is saying to us, and putting it into practice.'

OLD TESTAMENT		NEW TESTAMENT	
103.	Numbers 7	103.	Mark 6:1-29
104.	Numbers 8	104.	Mark 6:30-56
105.	Numbers 9, 10	105.	Mark 7:1-13
106.	Numbers 11	106.	Mark 7: 14-37
107.	Numbers 12	107.	Mark 8:1-21
108.	Numbers 13	108.	Mark 8:22-38
109.	Numbers 14, 15	109.	Mark 9:1-29
110.	Numbers 16	110.	Mark 9:30-50
111.	Numbers 17	111.	Mark 10:1-31
112.	Numbers 18	112.	Mark 10:32-52
113.	Numbers 19, 20	113.	Mark 11: 1-18
114.	Numbers 21	114.	Mark 11:19-33
115.	Numbers 22	115.	Mark 12:1-27
116.	Numbers 23	116.	Mark 12: 28-44
117.	Numbers 24, 25	117.	Mark 13:1-20
118.	Numbers 26	118.	Mark 13:21-37
119.	Numbers 27	119.	Mark 14:1-26
120.	Numbers 28	120.	Mark 14:27-53
121.	Numbers 29, 30	121.	Mark 14:54-72
122.	Numbers 31	122.	Mark 15:1-25
123.	Numbers 32	123.	Mark 15:26-47
124.	Numbers 33	124.	Mark 16
125.	Numbers 34, 35	125.	Romans 1
126.	Numbers 36	126.	Romans 2
127.	Psalm 13, 14	127.	Romans 3
128.	Psalm 15, 16	128.	Romans 4
129.	Deuteronomy 1	129.	Romans 5
130.	Deuteronomy 2	130.	Romans 6
131.	Deuteronomy 3	131.	Romans 7
132.	Deuteronomy 4, 5	132.	Romans 8:1-21
133.	Deuteronomy 6	133.	Romans 8:22-39
134.	Deuteronomy 7	134.	Romans 9:1-15
135.	Deuteronomy 8	135.	Romans 9:16-33
136.	Deuteronomy 9, 10	136.	Romans 10

YEAR

1

'Prayer should be woven into the fabric of the quiet time'.

OLD TESTAMENT		NEW TESTAMENT	
137.	**Deuteronomy 11**	**137.**	**Romans 11: 1-18**
138.	Deuteronomy 12	138.	Romans 11:19-36
139.	**Deuteronomy 13**	**139.**	**Romans 12**
140.	Deuteronomy 14, 15	140.	Romans 13
141.	**Deuteronomy 16**	**141.**	**Romans 14**
142.	Deuteronomy 17	142.	Romans 15:1-13
143.	**Deuteronomy 18**	**143.**	**Romans 15:14-33**
144.	Deuteronomy 19, 20	144.	Romans 16
145.	**Deuteronomy 21**	**145.**	**Luke 1:1-20**
146.	Deuteronomy 22	146.	Luke 1:21-38
147.	**Deuteronomy 23**	**147.**	**Luke 1:39-56**
148.	Deuteronomy 24, 25	148.	Luke 1:57-80
149.	**Deuteronomy 26**	**149.**	**Luke 2:1-24**
150.	Deuteronomy 27	150.	Luke 2:25-52
151.	**Deuteronomy 28**	**151.**	**Luke 3**
152.	Deuteronomy 29, 30	152.	Luke 4:1-30
153.	**Deuteronomy 31**	**153.**	**Luke 4:31-44**
154.	Deuteronomy 32	154.	Luke 5:1-16
155.	**Deuteronomy 33, 34**	**155.**	**Luke 5:17-39**
156.	Psalm 17, 18	156.	Luke 6:1-26
157.	**Psalm 19, 20**	**157.**	**Luke 6:27-49**
158.	Joshua 1	158.	Luke 7:1-30
159.	**Joshua 2**	**159.**	**Luke 7:31-50**
160.	Joshua 3	160.	Luke 8:1-25
161.	**Joshua 4,5**	**161.**	**Luke 8:26-56**
162.	Joshua 6	162.	Luke 9:1-36
163.	**Joshua 7**	**163.**	**Luke 9:37-62**
164.	Joshua8	164.	Luke 10:1-24
165.	**Joshua 9, 10**	**165.**	**Luke 10: 25-42**
166.	Joshua 11	166.	Luke 11:1-28
167.	**Joshua 12**	**167.**	**Luke 11:29-54**
168.	Joshua 13	168.	Luke 12:1-31
169.	**Joshua 14, 15**	**169.**	**Luke 12:32-59**
170.	Joshua 16	170.	Luke 13:1-22

YEAR 1

'The quiet time provides the opportunity for the Word to penetrate our hearts and transform our lives'.

OLD TESTAMENT		NEW TESTAMENT	
171.	Joshua 17	171.	Luke 13:23-35
172.	Joshua 18	172.	Luke 14:1-24
173.	Joshua 19, 20	173.	Luke 14:25-35
174.	Joshua 21	174.	Luke 15:1-10
175.	Joshua 22	175.	Luke 15:11-32
176.	Joshua 23, 24	176.	Luke 16
177.	Psalm 21, 22	177.	Luke 17:1-19
178.	Psalm 23, 24	178.	Luke 17: 20-37
179.	Judges 1	179.	Luke 18:1-23
180.	Judges 2	180.	Luke 18: 24-43
181.	Judges 3	181.	Luke 19:1-27
182.	Judges 4, 5	182.	Luke 19:28-48
183.	Judges 6	183.	Luke 20:1-26
184.	Judges 7	184.	Luke 20:27-47
185.	Judges 8	185.	Luke 21:1-19
186.	Judges 9, 10	186.	Luke 21:20-38
187.	Judges 11	187.	Luke 22: 1-20
188.	Judges 12	188.	Luke 22:21-46
189.	Judges 13	189.	Luke 22:47-71
190.	Judges 14,15	190.	Luke 23:1-25
191.	Judges 16	191.	Luke23:26-56
192.	Judges 17	192.	Luke 24:1-35
193.	Judges 18	193.	Luke 24:36-53
194.	Judges 19, 20	194.	1 Corinthians 1
195.	Judges 21	195.	1 Corinthians 2
196.	Psalm 25, 26	196.	1 Corinthians 3
197.	Psalm 27, 28	197.	1 Corinthians 4
198.	Ruth 1	198.	1 Corinthians 5
199.	Ruth 2	199.	1 Corinthians 6
200.	Ruth 3, 4	200.	1 Corinthians 7:1-19
201.	Psalm 29, 30	201.	1 Corinthians 7:20-40
202.	Psalm 31, 32	202.	1 Corinthians 8
203.	1 Samuel 1	203.	1 Corinthians 9
204.	1 Samuel 2	204.	1 Corinthians 10:1-18

YEAR **1**

'Stop and think about the privilege that you have been given! You are able to meet with your Creator, you are invited to encounter Almighty God, to hear from Him and worship Him'.

OLD TESTAMENT		NEW TESTAMENT	
205.	**1 Samuel 3**	**205.**	**1 Corinthians:10:19-33**
206.	1 Samuel 4, 5	206.	1 Corinthians 11:1-16
207.	**1 Samuel 6**	**207.**	**1 Corinthians:11:17-34**
208.	1 Samuel 7	208.	1 Corinthians 12
209.	**1 Samuel 8**	**209.**	**1 Corinthians 13**
210.	1 Samuel 9, 10	210.	1 Corinthians 14:1-20
211.	**1 Samuel 11**	**211.**	**1 Corinthians 14:21-40**
212.	1 Samuel 12	212.	1 Corinthians 15:1-28
213.	**1 Samuel 13**	**213.**	**1 Corinthians 15:29-58**
214.	1 Samuel 14, 15	214.	1 Corinthians 16
215.	**1 Samuel 16**	**215.**	**John 1:1-28**
216.	1 Samuel 17, 18	216.	John 1:29-51
217.	**1 Samuel 19**	**217.**	**John 2**
218.	1 Samuel 20, 21	218.	John 3:1-18
219.	**1 Samuel 22**	**219.**	**John 3:19-36**
220.	1 Samuel 23	220.	John 4:1-30
221.	**1 Samuel 24**	**221.**	**John 4:31-54**
222.	1 Samuel 25, 26	222.	John 5:1-24
223.	**1 Samuel 27**	**223.**	**John 5:25-47**
224.	1 Samuel 28	224.	John 6:1-21
225.	**1 Samuel 29**	**225.**	**John 6:22-44**
226.	1 Samuel 30,31	226.	John 6:45-71
227.	**Psalm 33, 34**	**227.**	**John 7:1-27**
228.	Psalm 35, 36	228.	John 7:28-53
229.	**2 Samuel 1**	**229.**	**John 8:1-27**
230.	2 Samuel 2	230.	John 8:28-59
231.	**2 Samuel 3**	**231.**	**John 9:1-23**
232.	2 Samuel 4,5	232.	John 9:24-41
233.	**2 Samuel 6**	**233.**	**John 10:1-23**
234.	2 Samuel 7	234.	John 10:24-42
235.	**2 Samuel 8**	**235.**	**John 11:1-29**
236.	2 Samuel 9, 10	236.	John 11:30-57
237.	**2 Samuel 11**	**237.**	**John 12:1-26**
238.	2 Samuel 12	238.	John 12:27-50

YEAR

1

*'God has
minted His will
into the coins
of promises,
and apart from
the coinage of
the realm, we
cannot know
God's mind or
heart'*

Michael Horton

OLD TESTAMENT		NEW TESTAMENT	
239.	**2 Samuel 13**	**239.**	**John 13:1-20**
240.	2 Samuel 14, 15	240.	John 13:21-38
241.	**2 Samuel 16**	**241.**	**John 14**
242.	2 Samuel 17	242.	John 15
243.	**2 Samuel 18**	**243.**	**John 16**
244.	2 Samuel 19, 20	244.	John 17
245.	**2 Samuel 21**	**245.**	**John 18:1-18**
246.	2 Samuel 22	246.	John 18:19-40
247.	**2 Samuel 23, 24**	**247.**	**John 19:1-22**
248.	Psalm 37, 38	248.	John 19:23-42
249.	**Psalm 39, 40**	**249.**	**John 20**
250.	1 Kings 1	250.	John 21
251.	**1 Kings 2**	**251.**	**2 Corinthians 1**
252.	1 Kings 3	252.	2 Corinthians 2
253.	**1 Kings 4, 5**	**253.**	**2 Corinthians 3**
254.	1 Kings 6	254.	2 Corinthians 4
255.	**1 Kings 7**	**255.**	**2 Corinthians 5**
256.	1 Kings 8	256.	2 Corinthians 6
257.	**1 Kings 9, 10**	**257.**	**2 Corinthians 7**
258.	1 Kings 11	258.	2 Corinthians 8
259.	**1 Kings 12**	**259.**	**2 Corinthians 9**
260.	1 Kings 13	260.	2 Corinthians 10
261.	**1 Kings 14, 15**	**261.**	**2 Corinthians 11:1-15**
262.	1 Kings 16	262.	2 Corinthians:11:16-33
263.	**1 Kings 17**	**263.**	**2 Corinthians 12**
264.	1 Kings 18	264.	2 Corinthians 13
265.	**1 Kings 19**	**265.**	**Galatians 1**
266.	1 Kings 20, 21	266.	Galatians 2
267.	**1 Kings 22**	**267.**	**Galatians 3**
268.	Psalm 41,42	268.	Galatians 4
269.	**Psalm 43, 44**	**269.**	**Galatians 5**
270.	2 Kings 1	270.	Galatians 6
271.	**2 Kings 2**	**271.**	**Ephesians 1**
272.	2 Kings 3	272.	Ephesians 2

YEAR

1

*'The Bible is
God's Word,
and we read it,
meditate on it,
and treasure it
because it is His
means of
communication
with us.'*

OLD TESTAMENT		NEW TESTAMENT	
273.	2 Kings 4, 5	273.	Ephesians 3
274.	2 Kings 6	274.	Ephesians 4
275.	2 Kings 7	275.	Ephesians 5:1-16
276.	2 Kings 8	276.	Ephesians 5:17-33
277.	2 Kings 9, 10	277.	Ephesians 6
278.	2 Kings 11	278.	Philippians 1
279.	2 Kings 12	279.	Philippians 2
280.	2 Kings 13	280.	Philippians 3
281.	2 Kings 14, 15	281.	Philippians 4
282.	2 Kings 16	282.	Colossians 1
283.	2 Kings 17	283.	Colossians 2
284.	2 Kings 18	284.	Colossians 3
285.	2 Kings 19, 20	285.	Colossians 4
286.	2 Kings 21	286.	1 Thessalonians 1
287.	2 Kings 22	287.	1 Thessalonians 2
288.	2 Kings 23	288.	1 Thessalonians 3
289.	2 Kings 24 ,25	289.	1 Thessalonians 4
290.	Psalm 45, 46	290.	1 Thessalonians 5
291.	Psalm 47, 48	291.	2 Thessalonians 1
292.	1 Chronicles 1	292.	2 Thessalonians 2
293.	1 Chronicles 2	293.	2 Thessalonians 3
294.	1 Chronicles 3	294.	1 Timothy 1
295.	1 Chronicles 4, 5	295.	1 Timothy 2
296.	1 Chronicles 6	296.	1 Timothy 3
297.	1 Chronicles 7	297.	1 Timothy 4
298.	1 Chronicles 8	298.	1 Timothy 5
299.	1 Chronicles 9, 10	299.	1 Timothy 6
300.	1 Chronicles 11	300.	2 Timothy 1
301.	1 Chronicles 12	301.	2 Timothy 2
302.	1 Chronicles 13	302.	2 Timothy 3
303.	1 Chronicles 14, 15	303.	2 Timothy 4
304.	1 Chronicles 16	304.	Titus 1
305.	1 Chronicles 17	305.	Titus 2
306.	1 Chronicles 18	306.	Titus 3

YEAR

1

'If the Bible is God's Word, we should not consider one part of it to be more or less the Word of God than another'.

OLD TESTAMENT		NEW TESTAMENT	
307.	**1 Chronicles 19, 20**	**307.**	**Philemon**
308.	1 Chronicles 21	308.	Hebrews 1
309.	**1 Chronicles 22**	**309.**	**Hebrews 2**
310.	1 Chronicles 23	310.	Hebrews 3
311.	**1 Chronicles 24, 25**	**311.**	**Hebrews 4**
312.	1 Chronicles 26	312.	Hebrews 5
313.	**1 Chronicles 27**	**313.**	**Hebrews 6**
314.	1 Chronicles 28, 29	314.	Hebrews 7
315.	**Psalm 49, 50**	**315.**	**Hebrews 8**
316.	Psalm 51, 52	316.	Hebrews 9
317.	**2 Chronicles 1**	**317.**	**Hebrews 10:1-18**
318.	2 Chronicles 2	318.	Hebrews 10:19-39
319.	**2 Chronicles 3**	**319.**	**Hebrews 11:1-19**
320.	2 Chronicles 4, 5	320.	Hebrews 11:20-40
321.	**2 Chronicles 6**	**321.**	**Hebrews 12**
322.	2 Chronicles 7	322.	Hebrews 13
323.	**2 Chronicles 8**	**323.**	**James 1**
324.	2 Chronicles 9	324.	James 2
325.	**2 Chronicles 10, 11**	**325.**	**James 3**
326.	2 Chronicles 12	326.	James 4
327.	**2 Chronicles 13**	**327.**	**James 5**
328.	2 Chronicles 14	328.	1 Peter 1
329.	**2 Chronicles 15, 16**	**329.**	**1 Peter 2**
330.	2 Chronicles 17	330.	1 Peter 3
331.	**2 Chronicles 18**	**331.**	**1 Peter 4**
332.	2 Chronicles 19	332.	1 Peter 5
333.	**2 Chronicles 20, 21**	**333.**	**2 Peter 1**
334.	2 Chronicles 22	334.	2 Peter 2
335.	**2 Chronicles 23**	**335.**	**2 Peter 3**
336.	2 Chronicles 24	336.	1 John 1
337.	**2 Chronicles 25, 26**	**337.**	**1 John 2**
338.	2 Chronicles 27	338.	1 John 3
339.	**2 Chronicles 28**	**339.**	**1 John 4**
340.	2 Chronicles 29	340.	1 John 5

YEAR
1

*'Let the fact
that you are
alone assert
itself. Give your
soul time to get
released from
the many
outward
things'*

O. Hallesby

OLD TESTAMENT		NEW TESTAMENT	
341.	**2 Chronicles 30, 31**	**341.**	**2 John**
342.	2 Chronicles 32	342.	3 John
343.	**2 Chronicles 33**	**343.**	**Jude**
344.	2 Chronicles 34	344.	Revelation 1
345.	**2 Chronicles 35, 36**	**345.**	**Revelation 2**
346.	Psalm 53, 54	346.	Revelation 3
		347.	**Revelation 4**
		348.	Revelation 5
		349.	**Revelation 6**
		350.	Revelation 7
		351.	**Revelation 8**
		352.	Revelation 9
		353.	**Revelation 10**
		354.	Revelation 11
		355.	**Revelation 12**
		356.	Revelation 13
		357.	**Revelation 14**
		358.	Revelation 15
		359.	**Revelation 16**
		360.	Revelation 17
		361.	**Revelation 18**
		362.	Revelation 19
		363.	**Revelation 20**
		364.	Revelation 21
		365.	**Revelation 22**

YEAR 2

'Our Christian Bookshops seem to be bursting at the seams with 'worship resources' but the best resource we have to hand is the Bible'.

OLD TESTAMENT	
1.	Psalm 55, 56
2.	Ezra 1, 2
3.	Ezra 3
4.	Ezra 4
5.	Ezra 5
6.	Ezra 6,7
7.	Ezra 8
8.	Ezra 9, 10
9.	Psalm 57, 58
10.	Psalm 59, 60
11.	Nehemiah 1
12.	Nehemiah 2
13.	Nehemiah 3
14.	Nehemiah 4,5
15.	Nehemiah 6
16.	Nehemiah 7
17.	Nehemiah 8
18.	Nehemiah 9, 10
19.	Nehemiah 11
20.	Nehemiah 12, 13
21.	Psalm 61, 62
22.	Psalm 63, 64
23.	Esther 1
24.	Esther 2.
25.	Esther 3
26.	Esther 4
27.	Esther 5, 6
28.	Esther 7
29.	Esther 8, 9, 10
30.	Psalm 65, 66
31.	Psalm 67, 68
32.	Job 1
33.	Job 2
34.	Job 3

NEW TESTAMENT	
1.	Matthew 1
2.	Matthew 2
3.	Matthew 3
4.	Matthew 4
5.	Matthew 5:1-26
6.	Matthew 5.27-48
7.	Matthew 6:1-18
8.	Matthew 6:19-34
9.	Matthew 7
10.	Matthew 8.1-17
11.	Matthew 8: 18-34
12.	Matthew 9: 1-17
13.	Matthew 9:18-38
14.	Matthew 10: 1-20
15.	Matthew 10:21-42
16.	Matthew 11
17.	Matthew 12: 1-23
18.	Matthew 12: 24-50
19.	Matthew 13: 1-30
20.	Matthew 13:31-58
21.	Matthew 14:1-21
22.	Matthew 14:22-36
23.	Matthew 15: 1-21
24.	Matthew 15: 22-39
25.	Matthew 16
26.	Matthew 17
27.	Matthew 18:1-20
28.	Matthew 18: 21-35
29.	Matthew 19
30.	Matthew 20:1-16
31.	Matthew 20:17-34
32.	Matthew 21: 1-22
33.	Matthew 21:23-46
34.	Matthew 22:1-22

YEAR

2

'When God fed
His people with
manna from
heaven, they
didn't need to
follow a
guidebook;
they just went
out and
collected it. Try
it, you'll have a
great surprise
in store!'

OLD TESTAMENT		NEW TESTAMENT	
35.	Job 4, 5	35.	Matthew 22:23-46
36.	Job 6	36.	Matthew23:1-22
37.	Job 7	37.	Matthew 23:23-39
38.	Job 8	38.	Matthew 24:1-28
39.	Job 9, 10	39.	Matthew 24:29-51
40.	Job 11	40.	Matthew 25:1-30
41.	Job 12	41.	Matthew 25:31-46
42.	Job 13	42.	Matthew 26:1-25
43.	Job 14, 15	43.	Matthew 26: 26-50
44.	Job 16	44.	Matthew 26: 51-75
45.	Job 17	45.	Matthew 27: 1-26
46.	Job 18	46.	Matthew 27:27-50
47.	Job 19 ,20	47.	Matthew 27: 51-66
48.	Job 21	48.	Matthew 28
49.	Job 22	49.	Acts 1
50.	Job 23	50.	Acts 2: 1-21
51.	Job 24, 25	51.	Acts 2: 22-47
52.	Job 26	52.	Acts 3
53.	Job 27	53.	Acts 4:1-22
54.	Job 28	54.	Acts 4:23-37
55.	Job 29, 30	55.	Acts 5:1-21
56.	Job 31	56.	Acts 5: 22-42
57.	Job 32	57.	Acts 6
58.	Job 33	58.	Acts 7:1-21
59.	Job 34, 35	59.	Acts 7:22-43
60.	Job 36	60.	Acts 7: 44-60
61.	Job 37	61.	Acts 8:1-25
62.	Job 38	62.	Acts 8:26-60
63.	Job 39, 40	63.	Acts 9:1-21
64.	Job 41	64.	Acts 9: 22-43
65.	Job 42	65.	Acts 10: 1-23
66.	Psalm 69, 70	66.	Acts 10: 24-48
67.	Psalm 71, 72	67.	Acts 11
68.	Proverbs 1, 2	68.	Acts 12

YEAR

2

'The words, 'in the beginning God', sound the theme that runs from Genesis to Revelation. The Bible is a book about God!'

OLD TESTAMENT		NEW TESTAMENT	
69.	**Proverbs 3**	**69.**	**Acts 13:1-25**
70.	Proverbs 4	70.	Acts 13:26-52
71.	**Proverbs 5, 6**	**71.**	**Acts 14**
72.	Proverbs 7	72.	Acts 15:1-21
73.	**Proverbs 8**	**73.**	**Acts 15: 22-41**
74.	Proverbs 9, 10	74.	Acts 16:1-21
75.	**Proverbs 11, 12**	**75.**	**Acts 16: 22-40**
76.	Proverbs 13	76.	Acts 17:1-15
77.	**Proverbs 14**	**77.**	**Acts 17: 16-34**
78.	Proverbs 15	78.	Acts 18
79.	**Proverbs 16. 17**	**79.**	**Acts 19:1-20**
80.	Proverbs 18	80.	Acts 19: 21-41
81.	**Proverbs 19**	**81.**	**Acts 20:1-16**
82.	Proverbs 20	82.	Acts 20:17-38
83.	**Proverbs 21, 22**	**83.**	**Acts 21: 1-17**
84.	Proverbs 23	84.	Acts 21:18-40
85.	**Proverbs 24**	**85.**	**Acts 22**
86.	Proverbs 25	86.	Acts 23:1-15
87.	**Proverbs 26, 27**	**87.**	**Acts 23:16-35**
88.	Proverbs 28	88.	Acts 24
89.	**Proverbs 29, 30**	**89.**	**Acts 25**
90.	Proverbs 31	90.	Acts 26
91.	**Psalm 73, 74**	**91.**	**Acts 27:1-26**
92.	Psalm 75, 76	92.	Acts 27:27-44
93.	**Ecclesiates 1**	**93.**	**Acts 28**
94.	Ecclesiates 2	94.	Mark 1:1-22
95.	**Ecclesiates 3**	**95.**	**Mark 1:23-45**
96.	Ecclesiates 4, 5	96.	Mark 2
97.	**Ecclesiates 6**	**97.**	**Mark 3:1-19**
98.	Ecclesiates 7	98.	Mark 3: 20-35
99.	**Ecclesiates 8**	**99.**	**Mark 4:1-20**
100.	Ecclesiates 9, 10	100.	Mark 4:21-41
101.	**Ecclesiates 11, 12**	**101.**	**Mark5:1-20**
102.	Psalm 77, 78	102.	Mark 5:21-43

YEAR **2**

'If Jesus is the centre of the universe, the goal of history and the focal point of the Bible, He must be the key to understanding God's Word.'

OLD TESTAMENT		NEW TESTAMENT	
103.	Psalm 79, 80	103.	Mark 6:1-29
104.	Song of Songs 1	104.	Mark 6:30-56
105.	Song of Songs 2	105.	Mark 7:1-13
106.	Song of Songs 3	106.	Mark 7: 14-37
107.	Song of Songs 4, 5	107.	Mark 8:1-21
108.	Song of Songs 6	108.	Mark 8:22-38
109.	Song of Songs 7, 8	109.	Mark 9:1-29
110.	Psalm 81, 82	110.	Mark 9:30-50
111.	Psalm 83, 84	111.	Mark 10:1-31
112.	Isaiah 1	112.	Mark 10:32-52
113.	Isaiah 2	113.	Mark 11: 1-18
114.	Isaiah 3	114.	Mark 11:19-33
115.	Isaiah 4,5	115.	Mark 12:1-27
116.	Isaiah 6	116.	Mark 12: 28-44
117.	Isaiah 7	117.	Mark 13:1-20
118.	Isaiah 8	118.	Mark 13:21-37
119.	Isaiah 9, 10	119.	Mark 14:1-26
120.	Isaiah 11	120.	Mark 14:27-53
121.	Isaiah 12	121.	Mark 14:54-72
122.	Isaiah 13	122.	Mark 15:1-25
123.	Isaiah 14, 15	123.	Mark 15:26-47
124.	Isaiah 16	124.	Mark 16
125.	Isaiah 17	125.	Romans 1
126.	Isaiah 18	126.	Romans 2
127.	Isaiah 19, 20	127.	Romans 3
128.	Isaiah 21	128.	Romans 4
129.	Isaiah 22	129.	Romans 5
130.	Isaiah 23	130.	Romans 6
131.	Isaiah 24, 25	131.	Romans 7
132.	Isaiah 26	132.	Romans 8:1-21
133.	Isaiah 27	133.	Romans 8:22-39
134.	Isaiah 28	134.	Romans 9:1-15
135.	Isaiah 29, 30	135.	Romans 9:16-33
136.	Isaiah 31	136.	Romans 10

YEAR

2

'We must stand
back, look at
the big picture,
and put the
passage we
read into the
context of the
great plan that
is unfolded
from Genesis to
Revelation'.

OLD TESTAMENT		NEW TESTAMENT	
137.	**Isaiah 32**	**137.**	**Romans 11: 1-18**
138.	Isaiah 33	138.	Romans 11:19-36
139.	**Isaiah 34, 35**	**139.**	**Romans 12**
140.	Isaiah 36	140.	Romans 13
141.	**Isaiah 37, 38**	**141.**	**Romans 14**
142.	Isaiah 39	142.	Romans 15:1-13
143.	**Isaiah 40, 41**	**143.**	**Romans 15:14-33**
144.	Isaiah 42	144.	Romans 16
145.	**Isaiah 43**	**145.**	**Luke 1:1-20**
146.	Isaiah 44	146.	Luke 1:21-38
147.	**Isaiah 45, 46**	**147.**	**Luke 1:39-56**
148.	Isaiah 47	148.	Luke 1:57-80
149.	**Isaiah 48**	**149.**	**Luke 2:1-24**
150.	Isaiah 49	150.	Luke 2:25-52
151.	**Isaiah 50, 51**	**151.**	**Luke 3**
152.	Isaiah 52	152.	Luke 4:1-30
153.	**Isaiah 53**	**153.**	**Luke 4:31-44**
154.	Isaiah 54	154.	Luke 5:1-16
155.	**Isaiah 55, 56**	**155.**	**Luke 5:17-39**
156.	Isaiah 57	156.	Luke 6:1-26
157.	**Isaiah 58**	**157.**	**Luke 6:27-49**
158.	Isaiah 59	158.	Luke 7:1-30
159.	**Isaiah 60, 61**	**159.**	**Luke 7:31-50**
160.	Isaiah 62	160.	Luke 8:1-25
161.	**Isaiah 63**	**161.**	**Luke 8:26-56**
162.	Isaiah 64	162.	Luke 9:1-36
163.	**Isaiah 65, 66**	**163.**	**Luke 9:37-62**
164.	Psalm 85, 86	164.	Luke 10:1-24
165.	**Psalm 87, 88**	**165.**	**Luke 10: 25-42**
166.	Jeremiah 1	166.	Luke 11:1-28
167.	**Jeremiah 2**	**167.**	**Luke 11:29-54**
168.	Jeremiah 3	168.	Luke 12:1-31
169.	**Jeremiah 4, 5**	**169.**	**Luke 12:32-59**
170.	Jeremiah 6	170.	Luke 13:1-22

YEAR

2

'Every part of
Jesus' life and
character
stands as an
example to us,
particularly the
way in which
He set time
aside to be
alone with His
Father.'

OLD TESTAMENT		NEW TESTAMENT	
171.	Jeremiah 7	171.	Luke 13:23-35
172.	Jeremiah 8	172.	Luke 14:1-24
173.	Jeremiah 9, 10	173.	Luke 14:25-35
174.	Jeremiah 11	174.	Luke 15:1-10
175.	Jeremiah 12	175.	Luke 15:11-32
176.	Jeremiah 13	176.	Luke 16
177.	Jeremiah 14, 15	177.	Luke 17:1-19
178.	Jeremiah 16	178.	Luke 17: 20-37
179.	Jeremiah 17	179.	Luke 18:1-23
180.	Jeremiah 18	180.	Luke 18: 24-43
181.	Jeremiah 19, 20	181.	Luke 19:1-27
182.	Jeremiah 21	182.	Luke 19:28-48
183.	Jeremiah 22	183.	Luke 20:1-26
184.	Jeremiah 23	184.	Luke 20:27-47
185.	Jeremiah 24, 25	185.	Luke 21:1-19
186.	Jeremiah 26	186.	Luke 21:20-38
187.	Jeremiah 27	187.	Luke 22: 1-20
188.	Jeremiah 28	188.	Luke 22:21-46
189.	Jeremiah 29,30	189.	Luke 22:47-71
190.	Jeremiah 31	190.	Luke 23:1-25
191.	Jeremiah 32	191.	Luke23:26-56
192.	Jeremiah 33	192.	Luke 24:1-35
193.	Jeremiah 34, 35	193.	Luke 24:36-53
194.	Jeremiah 36	194.	1 Corinthians 1
195.	Jeremiah 37	195.	1 Corinthians 2
196.	Jeremiah 38	196.	1 Corinthians 3
197.	Jeremiah 39, 40	197.	1 Corinthians 4
198.	Jeremiah 41	198.	1 Corinthians 5
199.	Jeremiah 42	199.	1 Corinthians 6
200.	Jeremiah 43	200.	1 Corinthians 7:1-19
201.	Jeremiah 44, 45	201.	1 Corinthians 7:20-40
202.	Jeremiah 46	202.	1 Corinthians 8
203.	Jeremiah 47 48	203.	1 Corinthians 9
204.	Jeremiah 49	204.	1 Corinthians 10:1-18

YEAR

2

*'Fewer and
fewer
Christians are
approaching
life with the
Berean
perspective.
They haven't
developed the
habit of
discerning or
applying
biblical
principles to
their daily
situations.'*

*John
MacArthur, Jr.*

OLD TESTAMENT		NEW TESTAMENT	
205.	**Jeremiah 50, 51**	**205.**	**1 Corinthians:10:19-33**
206.	Jeremiah 52	206.	1 Corinthians 11:1-16
207.	**Psalm 89, 90**	**207.**	**1 Corinthians:11:17-34**
208.	Psalm 91, 92	208.	1 Corinthians 12
209.	**Lamentations 1**	**209.**	**1 Corinthians 13**
210.	Lamentations 2	210.	1 Corinthians 14:1-20
211.	**Lamentations 3**	**211.**	**1 Corinthians 14:21-40**
212.	Lamentations 4, 5	212.	1 Corinthians 15:1-28
213.	**Psalm 93, 94**	**213.**	**1 Corinthians 15:29-58**
214.	Psalm 95, 96	214.	1 Corinthians 16
215.	**Ezekiel 1**	**215.**	**John 1:1-28**
216.	Ezekiel 2	216.	John 1:29-51
217.	**Ezekiel 3**	**217.**	**John 2**
218.	Ezekiel 4, 5	218.	John 3:1-18
219.	**Ezekiel 6**	**219.**	**John 3:19-36**
220.	Ezekiel 7	220.	John 4:1-30
221.	**Ezekiel 8**	**221.**	**John 4:31-54**
222.	Ezekiel 9, 10	222.	John 5:1-24
223.	**Ezekiel 11**	**223.**	**John 5:25-47**
224.	Ezekiel 12	224.	John 6:1-21
225.	**Ezekiel 13**	**225.**	**John 6:22-44**
226.	Ezekiel 14, 15	226.	John 6:45-71
227.	**Ezekiel 16, 17**	**227.**	**John 7:1-27**
228.	Ezekiel 18	228.	John 7:28-53
229.	**Ezekiel 19**	**229.**	**John 8:1-27**
230.	Ezekiel 20	230.	John 8:28-59
231.	**Ezekiel 21, 22**	**231.**	**John 9:1-23**
232.	Ezekiel 23	232.	John 9:24-41
233.	**Ezekiel 24**	**233.**	**John 10:1-23**
234.	Ezekiel 25	234.	John 10:24-42
235.	**Ezekiel 26, 27**	**235.**	**John 11:1-29**
236.	Ezekiel 28	236.	John 11:30-57
237.	**Ezekiel 29**	**237.**	**John 12:1-26**
238.	Ezekiel 30	238.	John 12:27-50

YEAR
2

*'We have been
trying to apply
machine-age
methods to our
relationship
with God. We
read our
chapter, have
our short
devotions and
rush away.'*

A.W. Tozer

	OLD TESTAMENT		NEW TESTAMENT
239.	**Ezekiel 31, 32**	**239.**	**John 13:1-20**
240.	Ezekiel 33	240.	John 13:21-38
241.	**Ezekiel 34**	**241.**	**John 14**
242.	Ezekiel 35	242.	John 15
243.	**Ezekiel 36, 37**	**243.**	**John 16**
244.	Ezekiel 38	244.	John 17
245.	**Ezekiel 39**	**245.**	**John 18:1-18**
246.	Ezekiel 40	246.	John 18:19-40
247.	**Ezekiel 41, 42**	**247.**	**John 19:1-22**
248.	Ezekiel 43	248.	John 19:23-42
249.	**Ezekiel 44**	**249.**	**John 20**
250.	Ezekiel 45	250.	John 21
251.	**Ezekiel 46, 47**	**251.**	**2 Corinthians 1**
252.	Ezekiel 48	252.	2 Corinthians 2
253.	**Psalm 97, 98, 99**	**253.**	**2 Corinthians 3**
254.	Psalm 100, 101,	254.	2 Corinthians 4
255.	**Daniel 1**	**255.**	**2 Corinthians 5**
256.	Daniel 2	256.	2 Corinthians 6
257.	**Daniel 3**	**257.**	**2 Corinthians 7**
258.	Daniel 4, 5	258.	2 Corinthians 8
259.	**Daniel 6**	**259.**	**2 Corinthians 9**
260.	Daniel 7	260.	2 Corinthians 10
261.	**Daniel 8, 9**	**261.**	**2 Corinthians 11:1-15**
262.	Daniel 10	262.	2 Corinthians:11:16-33
263.	**Daniel 11, 12**	**263.**	**2 Corinthians 12**
264.	Psalm 102, 103	264.	2 Corinthians 13
265.	**Psalm 104, 105,**	**265.**	**Galatians 1**
266.	Hosea 1	266.	Galatians 2
267.	**Hosea 2**	**267.**	**Galatians 3**
268.	Hosea 3	268.	Galatians 4
269.	**Hosea 4, 5**	**269.**	**Galatians 5**
270.	Hosea 6	270.	Galatians 6
271.	**Hosea 7**	**271.**	**Ephesians 1**
272.	Hosea 8	272.	Ephesians 2

YEAR

2

*'We have got
to be realistic
about our
wandering
minds; we can
train them, we
can increase
our
concentration,
but we will
fight a
constant battle
with stray
thoughts. Let's
remember that
it is a problem –
not a sin'*

OLD TESTAMENT		NEW TESTAMENT	
273.	**Hosea 9, 10**	**273.**	**Ephesians 3**
274.	Hosea 11	274.	Ephesians 4
275.	**Hosea 12**	**275.**	**Ephesians 5:1-16**
276.	Hosea 13, 14	276.	Ephesians 5:17-33
277.	**Psalm 106,107**	**277.**	**Ephesians 6**
278.	Psalm 108, 109	278.	Philippians 1
279.	**Joel 1**	**279.**	**Philippians 2**
280.	Joel 2,3	280.	Philippians 3
281.	**Psalm 110, 111**	**281.**	**Philippians 4**
282.	Psalm 112, 113	282.	Colossians 1
283.	**Amos 1**	**283.**	**Colossians 2**
284.	Amos 2	284.	Colossians 3
285.	**Amos 3**	**285.**	**Colossians 4**
286.	Amos 4, 5	286.	1 Thessalonians 1
287.	**Amos 6**	**287.**	**1 Thessalonians 2**
288.	Amos 7	288.	1 Thessalonians 3
289.	**Amos 8, 9**	**289.**	**1 Thessalonians 4**
290.	Psalm 114, 115	290.	1 Thessalonians 5
291.	**Psalm 116. 117**	**291.**	**2 Thessalonians 1**
292.	Psalm 118	292.	2 Thessalonians 2
293.	**Psalm 119:1-56**	**293.**	**2 Thessalonians 3**
294.	Psalm 119:57-112	294.	1 Timothy 1
295.	**Psalm 119:113-176**	**295.**	**1 Timothy 2**
296.	Obadiah	296.	1 Timothy 3
297.	**Jonah 1, 2**	**297.**	**1 Timothy 4**
298.	Jonah 3,4	298.	1 Timothy 5
299.	**Psalm 120, 121,**	**299.**	**1 Timothy 6**
300.	Psalm 122, 123	300.	2 Timothy 1
301.	**Micah 1**	**301.**	**2 Timothy 2**
302.	Micah 2	302.	2 Timothy 3
303.	**Micah 3**	**303.**	**2 Timothy 4**
304.	Micah 4,5	304.	Titus 1
305.	**Micah 6**	**305.**	**Titus 2**
306.	Micah 7	306.	Titus 3

DAILY READING PLAN

YEAR

2

'In time God does help us to overcome the turmoil and brings His peace and assurance to the situation ... The realisation dawns that He had been there all along, even in the darkest moments.'

Anon

	OLD TESTAMENT		NEW TESTAMENT
307.	**Psalm 124, 125**	**307.**	**Philemon**
308.	Psalm 126, 127	308.	Hebrews 1
309.	**Nahum 1**	**309.**	**Hebrews 2**
310.	Nahum 2,3	310.	Hebrews 3
311.	**Psalm 128, 129**	**311.**	**Hebrews 4**
312.	Psalm 130, 131	312.	Hebrews 5
313.	**Habakkuk 1**	**313.**	**Hebrews 6**
314.	Habakkuk 2,3	314.	Hebrews 7
315.	**Psalm 132, 133**	**315.**	**Hebrews 8**
316.	Psalm 134, 135	316.	Hebrews 9
317.	**Zephaniah 1**	**317.**	**Hebrews 10:1-18**
318.	Zephaniah 2, 3	318.	Hebrews 10:19-39
319.	**Psalm 136, 137**	**319.**	**Hebrews 11:1-19**
320.	Haggai 1	320.	Hebrews 11:20-40
321.	**Haggai 2**	**321.**	**Hebrews 12**
322.	Psalm 138, 139	322.	Hebrews 13
323.	**Zechariah 1**	**323.**	**James 1**
324.	Zechariah 2	324.	James 2
325.	**Zechariah 3**	**325.**	**James 3**
326.	Zechariah 4	326.	James 4
327.	**Zechariah 5**	**327.**	**James 5**
328.	Zechariah 6	328.	1 Peter 1
329.	**Zechariah 7**	**329.**	**1 Peter 2**
330.	Zechariah 8	330.	1 Peter 3
331.	**Zechariah 9**	**331.**	**1 Peter 4**
332.	Zechariah 10	332.	1 Peter 5
333.	**Zechariah 11**	**333.**	**2 Peter 1**
334.	Zechariah 12	334.	2 Peter 2
335.	**Zechariah 13**	**335.**	**2 Peter 3**
336.	Zechariah 14	336.	1 John 1
337.	**Psalm 140**	**337.**	**1 John 2**
338.	Malachi 1	338.	1 John 3
339.	**Malachi 2**	**339.**	**1 John 4**
340.	Malachi 3	340.	1 John 5

YEAR

2

*'When the
going gets
tough, and the
Christian life
gets dry, we
can encourage
ourselves with
the realisation
that God loves
us, and is more
eager to meet
with us than
we are to meet
with Him.'*

OLD TESTAMENT	
341.	**Malachi 4**
342.	Psalm 141, 142
343.	**Psalm 143, 144**
344.	Psalm 145, 146
345.	**Psalm 147, 148**
346.	Psalm149, 150

NEW TESTAMENT	
341.	**2 John**
342.	3 John
343.	**Jude**
344.	Revelation 1
345.	**Revelation 2**
346.	Revelation 3
347.	**Revelation 4**
348.	Revelation 5
349.	**Revelation 6**
350.	Revelation 7
351.	**Revelation 8**
352.	Revelation 9
353.	**Revelation 10**
354.	Revelation 11
355.	**Revelation 12**
356.	Revelation 13
357.	**Revelation 14**
358.	Revelation 15
359.	**Revelation 16**
360.	Revelation 17
361.	**Revelation 18**
362.	Revelation 19
363.	**Revelation 20**
364.	Revelation 21
365.	**Revelation 22**

Also from Day One

A unique new
Bible devotional
with a difference

365 days with Spurgeon

A unique daily Bible devotional containing powerful insights from C.H. Spurgeon's Park Street Pulpit

384 pages
Paperback   £9.99
Casebound   £11.99

Charles Haddon Spurgeon possessed a deep and abiding reverence for the authority of God's Written Word (the Bible) to the end of his days. His application of God's eternal truths which he found there and his recognition of how the ensnaring affairs of daily life both wound and affect believers, rightly places him as a spiritual giant in the eyes of many Christians.

In this volume, it is clear that Spurgeon had an amazing capacity for anticipating the daily crouching of 'sin at the door' of every Christian, together with the biblical antidote. Here we have absolute confirmation that his was no late

For further information, call or write to us:

01372 728 300

flowering of Godly wisdom. Here, from the archive of Spurgeon's Park Street sermons (long before his well-known days at London's more famous Metropolitan Tabernacle) we have pearls of Biblical wisdom indeed.

What is particularly striking, however, is how incredibly appropriate they are to the ears of the contemporary Christian in need of genuine spiritual understanding. As the new millennium fast approaches, all Christians would benefit from hearing the words of such a giant of the Word. One who understood only too well the sinful nature and motives of contemporary society in search of meaning. More than that, Spurgeon provides insight into the contemporary 'worldly-wise' mind and its wearying, pressurising effect on the soul of the believing Christian living in its midst.

If it is food and medicine for the soul and wisdom for the mind which you seek, then you will find spoonfuls in these pages.

* **A unique daily Bible devotional containing powerful insights from C.H. Spurgeon's Park Street Pulpit.**

* **Contains a helpful scripture index.**

* **Available in case binding or paperback.**

* **All editions have sewn binding and will give years of service.**

ISBN 0 902548 83 2 Paperback
ISBN 0 902548 84 0 Casebound

In Europe: ++ 44 1372 728 300

In North America: 011 44 1372 728 300

Day One 3 Epsom Business Park Kiln Lane Epsom Surrey KT17 1JF England

E–Mail: ldos.dayone@ukonline.co.uk

Also from Day One

Why Lord?
The Book of Job for today

Gary Benfold

Foreword by Stuart Olyott

Paperback
152 pages   £6.99

Job was a godly man who could not
understand why he had to suffer so much.
His friends could not come up with any
satisfying answers. Not even God answered
his questions. And yet it was in listening to
God that he was freed from turmoil and
found peace of heart.
Gary Benfold skilfully guides us through
the book's main movement and themes,
constantly underlining how it speaks to us
today. Brilliant summaries, teaching from
elsewhere in scripture, concrete examples,
varied and lively illustrations, all combine
to drive the lessons home.
Why Lord? is thoroughly biblical,
theologically rigorous and filled with
practical help. It points us to Christ,
glories in his cross, and convinces us that it
is always safe to trust the living God who,
in his wisdom, often chooses not to
explain himself. It is just the sort of book
that so many of us need.

Reference: WHY
ISBN 0 902548 76 X

Theophany: Close Encounters
with The Son of God

Jonathan Stephen

Foreword by Michael Bentley

Paperback
160 pages   £6.99

This book will not only help those
believers who see little value in the Old
Testament, but it will show that the Lord
Jesus Christ is very clearly displayed in the
book of Genesis as he appears to a number
of the patriarchs. It will also be a great
strength to those who have known and
valued the Word of God for many years.

Reference: CLO
ISBN 0 902548 82 4

"An easy-to-read up-to-date
application of the truth of
God which will bring
enrichment to many
people".

Michael Bentley

For further information about these and other Day One titles, call or write to us:

01372 728 300

In Europe: ++ 44 1372 728 300

In North America: 011 44 1372 728 300

Day One   3 Epsom Business Park Kiln Lane Epsom Surrey KT17 1JF England

E–Mail: ldos.dayone@ukonline.co.uk